SNAPREVISE

SnapRevise Text Guide:
A Christmas Carol
by Charles Dickens

Lara Renata Partridge

InStudent Education UK Ltd owner of SnapRevise® trademark.
43 Priston Close, Worle, BS22 7FL, Weston-Super-Mare, United Kingdom

www.snaprevise.co.uk

Title: A Christmas Carol by Charles Dickens Text Guide
ISBN: 978-1-917424-11-0

Published by InStudent Education UK Ltd CN 15550989 under licence from InStudent Publishing Pty Ltd.
ACN 624 188101

Preface

My name is Lara Renata Partridge and I graduated with top scores in English, Literature, and Ancient History. Over the years I have also won several writing prizes. I am currently studying Law/Arts (Honours) at Monash University, where I am majoring in Italian and minoring in Literary Studies. I have also worked extensively as a high school tutor.

A Christmas Carol by Charles Dickens, published in 1843, has been a popular and much-loved Christmas tale for many decades. Upon first glance, the novella may seem to be a simple Christmas story designed to entertain children and adults alike. Indeed, it has been re-adapted into illustrated children's books, films, cartoons, plays, and several other media. As a result, many students may already be familiar with this infamous tale – even if not in its original novella form.

However, beyond its surface level appearance, *A Christmas Carol* preaches several important messages at its core about human nature and the broader significance of Christmas – beyond decorations, decadent food, and gifts.

In today's modern 21st century, where the Christian tradition of Christmas is often perceived as a largely commercialised and materialistic occasion, *A Christmas Carol* serves as a timeless reminder of Christmas' essential origins and the moral values it expounds to Christians and non-Christians alike.

Thus, it is the aim of this Text Guide to shed an analytical light on a perceived festive and seasonal tale, which has more to offer beyond the theme of Christmas in its most simple and superficial sense.

— Lara Renata Partridge

Contents

Section 1

Nutshell Summary

Charles Dickens's 1843 novella, *A Christmas Carol*, begins with the death of Jacob Marley (Ebenezer Scrooge's former associate). The two men had operated a firm together known as 'Scrooge and Marley.' Scrooge is now left as the sole **proprietor.**

Scrooge's nephew Fred enters the **countinghouse** on the 24th of December, Christmas Eve, wishing Scrooge a merry Christmas. The two men engage in a debate over the merits and demerits of Christmas, with Scrooge bitterly denouncing it as a "humbug." Scrooge firmly rejects his nephew's invitation to dine at his house on Christmas Day.

Two charitable gentlemen then enter the countinghouse, seeking donations for the "Poor and **destitute**" of London. Scrooge resentfully refuses to offer his funds, despite his renowned wealth within the city.

Scrooge's third interaction occurs with his employed clerk Bob Cratchit. Bob belongs to a poor family of humble means, who struggle to support their sickly child Tiny Tim. Scrooge unwillingly permits Cratchit the day off on Christmas, angrily commenting on the injustice of paying "a day's wages for no work."

The introduction of the novella thus sets up the characterisation of Scrooge: **an ageing, wealthy, selfish, and bitter old man who fails to see the value and joy in Christmas.**

Upon returning home, Scrooge is then confronted by the ghost of his old companion Marley, who warns Scrooge of the perils of living a **frugal** and uncompassionate life. Marley's ghost himself is weighted with heavy chains of metal, symbolising the consequences in the afterlife of pursuing a life of egotism and opportunism.

Though initially unconvinced by the ghost's warning, Scrooge is told that he will be visited by three spirits, sent to teach a moral lesson to which Scrooge is blind.

Scrooge is first frequented by the Ghost of Christmas Past, who takes him through various events from his childhood and adulthood. Scrooge, who at first is presented to the reader as an entirely grave and unemotional character, is sympathetic towards these memories, reminiscing on events he had once suppressed in his mind.

Proprietor: the owner of a business or property.

Countinghouse: where financial records were traditionally kept (like an old fashioned accountant's office!).

Destitute: devoid or deprived, impoverished.

Frugal: not wanting to spend money; being thrifty or economical and living cheaply.

He is then confronted by the Ghost of Christmas Present, who shows Scrooge the celebrations of various Londoners on Christmas Day. Here, Scrooge is awakened to the community members' unsympathetic opinions of him, viewing his harsh nature as cruel and oppressive.

Lastly, Scrooge is guided by the Ghost of Christmas Yet To Come, and is horrifically confronted by the future prospect of his very own death. Scrooge is perturbed by this final imagery, pleading with the spirit and pledging to amend his ways and treat Christmas with the same joy and generosity that the ghost itself preaches.

Benevolence: goodwill and kindness.

Scrooge is surprised to awaken on Christmas Day with the teachings of the spirits firmly ingrained in his conscience. He pledges to amend his previous wrongdoings, and to go forth with a new outlook of **benevolence**, sending the "prize turkey" to the Cratchit household, donating a generous sum to the "Poor and destitute" of London, and celebrating with his nephew's family.

The novella thus concludes with an idealistic perception of what Christmas should be: **a celebration of thanksgiving and prosperity,** devoid of the selfishness and spite previously fostered by Scrooge.

Section 2

Background Information

Charles Dickens's novella *A Christmas Carol* was published on the 19th of December in 1843, and is set in London in the Victorian era. This section will briefly explore Dickens's biography, as well as all the contextual information you need to know to study this text.

Charles Dickens

Charles Dickens was an English writer and social critic whose literary works received unprecedented attention and success during his lifetime. As such, Dickens has earned his place as one of the most successful and talented novelists in the British literary canon.

Dickens was born on the southern coast of England in 1812, growing up during Queen Victoria's reign. He had somewhat of a tumultuous childhood, with his father going to prison for debt, which ended in Dickens leaving school to work in the factories as a young boy. This is widely considered an important event in Dickens's life, that had a large impact on his world view. Despite his rough early years, he finished school and went on to work in a number of jobs in law and journalism, eventually being asked to write a serial narrative called *The Pickwick Papers* in 1836. This turned out to be quite a success, and began his literary career. The serialisation of his novels, including the celebrated *Oliver Twist*, became the most popular mode of novel publication in Victorian England.

Creating works such as *Great Expectations*, *A Tale of Two Cities*, and *David Copperfield*, Dickens was highly regarded as one of the greatest, and certainly most popular, novelists of his time. His novels had plenty for all to enjoy and included satire, humour, and his infamous ability to observe and scrutinise character and society. The common literary themes in Dickens's works have given rise to the term 'Dickensian,' which is used to describe something that parallels his works (e.g. in its reflection of poor social conditions, or comically dislikeable characters).

Why did Dickens write *A Christmas Carol*?

Charles Dickens was first inspired to author his novella *A Christmas Carol* on his travels to Northern England, where he spoke at the Manchester Athenaeum (a **philanthropic** organisation designed to aid the working poor). The lower classes were significantly uneducated, powerless, exploited by the rich and middle class, and neglected by society at large. Dickens participated in an event held in October of 1843 designed to raise money for the Athenaeum. He spoke alongside the prominent politicians Benjamin Disraeli and Richard Cobden.

Philanthropic: encouraging the welfare of others through charity and generosity.

Already a well-known and illustrious novelist, Dickens's time in Manchester alerted him to the need to explore what he perceived to be **England's two greatest crises: want and ignorance.** Indeed, Dickens personified these attributes in his novella with the two children that tug hauntingly on the robe of the Ghost of Christmas Present. These so-called 'threats' of want and ignorance faced the slums of England, growing ever so rapidly in the nation's newly industrialised and urbanised cities. Only six weeks after this **epiphanic** revelation, *A Christmas Carol* was completed.

Epiphany: a sudden deep or enlightened understanding of something.

Dickens continued to write what he dubbed his 'Christmas Books' for many years, however none of these works have achieved the same literary supremacy as *A Christmas Carol.*

Victorian Era

Victorian era: the period when Queen Victoria ruled England, characterised by the Industrial revolution, new scientific concepts, greater national prosperity, and new political ideals.

The **Victorian era** (1837–1901) was a dynamic time of political reform and social change characterised by a railway and industrial boom and the invention of the first phone and telegraph. Many were migrating to the cities at this time as opportunities increased. However the quick rise in population led to increased poverty, and slums sprung up within the cities. The poor worked long, strict hours in polluted factories, while the middle and upper classes continued to exploit the manpower of this working class. As such, the Victorian era was certainly a prosperous one, yet it was **underscored by the struggle and fatigue of Britain's poor.**

In *A Christmas Carol*, Dickens opposes the reigning supremacy of the rich and prosperous (broadly represented by Scrooge). Simultaneously, he encourages sympathy and compassion towards the less fortunate, epitomised by individuals like the Cratchits (and Tiny Tim in particular). Therefore, *A Christmas Carol* is in many ways a harsh critique of Victorian society.

The Victorian era was also one of the most significant periods in history to influence the way Christmas is celebrated today. Before Queen Victoria's reign began in 1837, the **archetypal** Christmas festivities of Santa Claus, Christmas crackers, Christmas cards, and work holidays remained very much foreign. However, Christmas was forever changed during this period as a result of the first Industrial Revolution and the prosperity it brought for the country.

Archetypal: the expected or established way something should be.

Due to the newfound wealth generated by machinery in this period, time off work became more common and gifts became less expensive, hence Christmas became more like we know it today. The introduction of new railway systems also affected Christmas festivities, allowing workers to easily travel home, and slashing the cost of sending cards to loved ones, hence Christmas cards were popularised.

Christianity

Charles Dickens was considered to be a staunch Christian. As such, it is no surprise that *A Christmas Carol* is often interpreted as a **non-secular** tale. It has frequently been described as a **Christian allegory,** which celebrates not only the religious notions of the Nativity and the Epiphany, but the broader narrative of Christ: from the Nativity to the Resurrection.

Scrooge's **odyssey** for example, occurs over three nights (though his journey with the three spirits is often condensed into one night in cartoon and film adaptions). It is only by the sheer miracle of the spirits that Scrooge arises after these ordeals on Christmas morning. This may be interpreted as a parallel to Christ rising on the third day, ascending into heaven, just as Scrooge ascends from selfishness to goodwill.

Likewise, the characters make several **biblical and religious allusions** throughout the novella. Perhaps most significant is Tiny Tim, who professes that he is glad that the churchgoers saw him with his crutch on his way home, so that the Londoners may remember "on Christmas Day who made lame beggars walk and blind men see."

Likewise, Fred champions Christmas "apart from the **veneration** due its sacred name and origin, if anything belonging to it can be apart from that, as a good time." Scrooge perhaps serves as the **antithesis** to enshrined Christian values. His partner Jacob Marley bemoans "not to know that any Christian spirit will find its mortal life too short for its vast means of usefulness." So too, does he lament his failure to follow "that blessed star which led the Wise Men to a poor abode."

The narrator, perhaps echoing the voice of Dickens himself, professes the merits of being child-like at Christmas, "when its mighty founder was a child himself." Dickens thus establishes a **parallel between Scrooge's own moral awakening, and the epiphanic Christian origins of Christmas.**

Non-secular: involving religious or spiritual matters.

Allegory: a story with another underlying meaning.

Odyssey: a long adventure or journey.

Allusion: an indirect reference to something.

Veneration: showing great respect or reverence.

Antithesis: the complete opposite of something.

Inspiration

In many ways, Charles Dickens's *A Christmas Carol* is influenced significantly by Dante Alighieri's seminal narrative poem, ***La Divina Commedia* (*The Divine Comedy*),** formally published in 1472.

Dante Alighieri (1265–1321) was a famous Italian poet, writer, and philosopher, most renowned for his *The Divine Comedy* (although he also produced several other successful works). Dante is often recognised as the father of Italian literature, and the Italian language at large.

On a simple level, *The Divine Comedy* explores the three realms of **Hell, Purgatory, and Heaven** (just as *A Christmas Carol* considers the **past, present, and future**). In *The Divine Comedy* the narrator (and pilgrim), perceived to be Dante himself, is lead through these realms by two guides – Beatrice, who represents divine faith and grace, and Virgil, the Latin poet who symbolises human reason. This can be paralleled to the way in which Scrooge, a 'pilgrim' of sorts like Dante, is guided by the three spirits who each proffer a different moral teaching.

Dickens was thus inspired by the structural elements of Dante's *The Divine Comedy*, as well as his strong Christian allusions (see previous). It is perhaps these timeless themes, of religion and human nature, which make both Dante and Dickens so successful.

KEY POINT :

Please note that for the purposes of studying this text at school, that no knowledge is required of Dante. This discussion merely raises some interesting explanatory points which may elucidate the various facets of inspiration open to Dickens.

Section 3

Chapter-by-Chapter Analysis

Overview

A Christmas Carol is divided into five 'staves,' which can be considered as chapters. The fact that Dickens chose to label these as 'staves' is significant, and bears a strong relationship with the meaning conveyed by the title. *A Christmas Carol,* as the name suggests, refers to a Christmas song with lyrics, often religious in nature and sung in groups. Moreover, a stave is in fact a musical term (also known as a staff). It is defined as a set of five parallel lines on which musical notes are written in order to indicate their pitch. As such, Dickens establishes a parallel between his novella and a literal Christmas carol, whereby each of the chapters acts as a part of the song.

Christmas carols are generally characterised by their timeless and memorable nature, and their communication of some moral or human message or **ethos.** They are often sung in unison, establishing an air of harmony. Thus, Dickens perhaps intends for his tale to be preserved through time as a well-known fable, common to the ears of all who hear it.

Ethos: a set of belief systems.

Stave 1: Marley's Ghost

Summary

The tale *A Christmas Carol* begins on the cold and frosty night of Christmas Eve in Scrooge's countinghouse.

Dickens opens the novella with the blunt and pragmatic remark "Marley was dead," alerting the audience to the death of Scrooge's business partner Jacob Marley seven years prior. The protagonist, Ebenezer Scrooge, is then introduced to the reader as an obviously dull and bitter man, described as an "old sinner" devoid of any "warmth."

The scene begins with the entrance of Scrooge's clerk and nephew, Fred, who comments on the "cheerful" and "merry" nature of Christmas. Fred's exaltation of Christmas is greeted with a "morose" **vitriol** by Scrooge, who **castigates** it as a "humbug." Scrooge thus angrily rejects his nephew's invitation to dine with his family on Christmas Day, dismissing him with a curt "good afternoon."

Vitriol: bitter criticism or malice.

Scrooge is then greeted in his countinghouse by two gentlemen seeking donations for the "Poor and destitute" of London. It is this interaction, which points most towards Scrooge's lack of charitably and empathy towards the poor. Just as he dismissed his nephew, so too does he dismiss the good-doers, cruelly suggesting that the "hundreds and thousands" of London's poor be sent to the "prisons" and "Union workhouses."

Castigate: to attack, critique, condemn, or disparage someone or something.

Scrooge is subsequently frequented by a Christmas caroller, yet Scrooge's swiftness of action in "seiz[ing] the ruler" sends the singer away in acute terror. Scrooge's final interaction then occurs with his employee, Bob Cratchit, to whom Scrooge reluctantly grants Christmas Day off work. Scrooge comments on the **antithetical** idea of paying his clerks on a day where no actual work is performed, cruelly shunning Cratchit's status as a poor and dedicated member of the working class, who works tirelessly to support his humble family and his crippled and sickly son Tiny Tim.

Antithetical: opposing, contrasting, or contrary to something.

Upon Cratchit's departure, Scrooge locks up his countinghouse and returns home, he is shocked to see what appears to be the ghost of his former partner Jacob Marley, weighted with heavy chains, walking through the door towards him. Scrooge is at first sceptical of the ghost, yet quickly learns of the haunting news it brings.

Marley informs Scrooge that he is to be visited by three spirits, each of which will transport him through different realms of time: Christmas Past, Christmas Present, and Christmas Future. Marley warns that men of his and Scrooge's conviction are "doomed to wander through the world." Marley's remorse unsettles Scrooge, yet he remains sceptical as to the truths it speaks. The stave ends with Scrooge collapsing into a deep slumber, yet to be woken by the Ghost of Christmas Past in the following chapter.

Analysis

The first stave serves the fundamental purpose of portraying the egotism, insensitivity, greed, and unkindness of Scrooge's character. It is this **skilful characterisation** that allows for such a **stark dichotomy in Scrooge's conviction** by the end of the novella.

By commencing the stave with the knowledge of Marley's death, Dickens hints at the impending intrusion of Marley's terrifying spectre into Scrooge's home. The narrator empathetically repeats the assertion, "Old Marley was dead as a door-nail." whereby the **alliteration** of the **plosive** 'd' augments the forthright and **didactic** tone of the statement, removing any chance for hesitance or denial. The irony is, of course, that the "dead" Marley will appear to Scrooge in the unsettling form of his ghost within only a matter of paragraphs.

Alliteration: the repetition of the same letter at the beginning of words close to one another.

Plosive: certain consonants which 'explode' out of the mouth when spoken (specifically t, k, p, d, g, and b).

Didactic: instructive, designed to teach a moral lesson.

Like Scrooge, it is clear that Marley was a man of voluntary isolation and greed. The narrator professes that Scrooge was "his sole executor, his sole administrator, his sole assign, his sole residuary legatee, his sole friend and his sole mourner." Here, the **repetition of "sole"** almost becomes a chant, **emphasising the isolating life of the archetypically insular 'rich man'.** Both Scrooge and Marley have no friends nor confidants. Scrooge's status as Marley's "sole mourner," also presages the scene he is yet to witness alongside the Ghost of Christmas Yet to Come, where Scrooge's hypothetical death sparks no mourning or grief within the city. Marley had one mourner, but Scrooge however, may have none.

Even so, it is clear that Scrooge's mourning over his partner was merely superficial. Indeed, "he was not so dreadfully cut up by the sad event," but instead, mourned the loss of a successful business partner who raked in profitable funds to their business.

In establishing the importance of the reader's knowledge of Marley's death, Dickens alludes to Elizabethan playwright William Shakespeare's tragedy *Hamlet*: "If we were not perfectly convinced that Hamlet's father died before the play began, there would be nothing more remarkable in his taking a stroll at night." In *Hamlet*, the tragic hero (i.e. the character of Hamlet), is visited by the ghost of his father (King Hamlet), who implores him to avenge his death. Without the ghost's heed, many of the play's central events would not have unfolded. As such, Dickens establishes a parallel between the significance of Marley's death and King Hamlet's ghost, **foreshadowing** once more the spectre which is yet to haunt Scrooge.

Foreshadow: a literary technique used by an author to hint at events yet to come in the story.

From the very opening of the stave, Dickens portrays Ebenezer Scrooge and Jacob Marley as incredibly alike figures: **both characterised by their greed.** Indeed, the narrator reveals that Scrooge "answered to both names" (Scrooge and Marley) when wrongly addressed by customers. To Scrooge, "it was all the same to him." The fact that Scrooge pragmatically accepts the identity of his partner suggests his sole concern with profit and business. So long as he receives new customers, he cares not what they call him.

Dickens writes in the **third person omniscient voice** (i.e. using he/she rather than I/you), and possesses full knowledge of each of the character's thoughts and emotions. He is able to access the opinions of each character in the world of the text. Dickens also often makes use of **free indirect speech,** whereby the narrator adopts the 'voice' or 'manner of speaking' of one of the characters in the texts, whilst still writing as the narrator. As such, Dickens's narrative voice is permeated by a **dynamic variety of tones,** and is often pervaded by **exclamatory statements** – ascribing a forthrightness and dynamism to the tone.

Exclamatory statement: a statement concluded with an exclamation mark.

As such, much of the first few paragraphs of the novella (devoid of any dialogue between characters) adopts the free indirect speech of a perceived Londoner who is acquainted with Scrooge's fixed and deplorable ways. The narrator characterises Scrooge as a "squeezing, wrenching, grasping, scraping, clutching, covetous, old sinner!" This list of unfavourable adjectives are delivered in an exclamatory way, almost as though the narrator were out of breath. The connotations of each adjective tap into the depths of Scrooge's deficient morals. Moreover, the exclamatory nature of the statement ascribes it with a firm definitiveness, as though the observation were a universal **axiom,** and cannot be rebutted.

Axiom: a rule that cannot be proven but is taken as truth – usually in mathematics.

In the initial paragraphs of the stave, Dickens establishes a parallel between the literal coldness of the wintry weather, and the metaphor of the "cold within" Scrooge's conscious, which "froze his old features, nipped his pointed nose... and spoke out shrewdly in his grating voice." The metaphor is extended with the "frosty rime... on his head, and on his eyebrows, and his wiry chin. He carried his own low temperature always about with him." Scrooge's unsympathetic and insensitive nature is thus established – as biting and bitter as the winter cold. Scrooge is almost rendered void of his human characteristics, with the notion that "external heat and cold had little influence on" him. Indeed, "no warmth could warm, no wintry weather chill him." Scrooge is therefore **objectified** as a soulless object.

Objectified: to view a person as no more than a thing without valid opinions or rights to their own.

The narrator then continues with imagery of "blind men's dogs" who "would tug their owners into doorways" upon seeing Scrooge approach. This reflects Scrooge's reception by the city of London as he is perceived as an oppressive individual who, as a result, is isolated in his interactions. Yet this isolation is most welcome to Scrooge, it was "the very thing he liked." The free indirect speech, "but what did Scrooge care," communicates Scrooge's air of dismissal and self-satisfaction. He is ultimately disinterested in appearing likeable to others.

The story then begins in earnest at Scrooge's countinghouse on Christmas Eve. Dickens sets up Scrooge's firm to be viewed as confined and clinical, whereby his clerk's work conditions are predictably far inferior to Scrooge's. His clerk, Bob Cratchit, works in a "little cell" likened to a "tank." His fire is so "much smaller [than Scrooge's] that it looked like one coal." Of course, Bob is prohibited from adding to it, as Scrooge keeps watch over the extra coal.

Juxtaposition: a technique that contrasts two things against one another to emphasise their differences.

Caustic: corrosive or scathing.

Dickens then interrupts this 'scene setting' with the entrance of Scrooge's nephew Fred, who in a "cheerful voice" bodes scrooge a Merry Christmas. Fred's gleeful expression serves as a stark **juxtaposition** to the bitter and **caustic** attitude the reader has seen of Scrooge. Unlike Scrooge's icy and frigid demeanour, Fred is by contrast, "heated... with rapid walking," his body "in a glow," his eyes "sparkl[ing]" and his breath "smoked." This **dichotomy between coldness and warmth,** thus points towards the broader gulf which lies between Scrooge and the Londoners at large.

Scrooge impatiently questions Fred's right "to be merry," commenting that he is "poor enough" to negate such a gleeful outlook. Fred happily questions Scrooge's reason "to be morose" when he has plenty of money. Here, **Dickens establishes a further dichotomy between the rich and the poor.** Whilst Fred is of humble means, he is nevertheless merry, undeterred by Scrooge's vitriol. Yet, though Scrooge is wealthy and prosperous, he dwells in a chasm of bitterness. Dickens thus suggests, that **wealth is not the antidote to humanity's problems** nor to unhappiness. Rather, he renders wealth insignificant in the pursuit of contentment. This is also, perhaps, a broader critique on Victorian society.

Scrooge rationalises his hatred of Christmas by arguing that on Christmas one must "pay... bills without money" and that time passes yet you aren't "an hour richer." He thus seeks material and commercial value in everything he pursues. Even more cruelly, he declares that "every idiot who goes about with 'Merry Christmas' on his lips, should be boiled with his own pudding, and buried with a stake of holly through his heart." This association of Christmas with violence and death is indicative of the bleak lens through which he perceives it.

Fred counters Scrooge's **diatribe** with a romanticised depiction of the Christmas ideal. It is perhaps in this paragraph, that Dickens indicates to his reader the broader message of *A Christmas Carol,* in its endorsement of Christmas values. Most notably, Fred espouses that Christmas is the sole time of year when "men and women seem by one consent to open their shut-up hearts freely, and to think of people below them as if they really were fellow-passengers to the grave, and not another race of creatures bound to other journeys." Ironically, Scrooge does exactly this by the conclusion of the novella by unlocking his "shut-up heart" and liberally sharing a generosity which had previously been untapped. However, initially Scrooge is unmoved by this reflection, and ends the encounter with his nephew by declining his invitation to dine at his family's house on Christmas Day.

Diatribe: a verbal attack against something.

Upon the subsequent entrance of two charitable gentleman seeking donations for the "Poor and destitute" of London, Scrooge sarcastically muses whether there are "no prisons" or "Union workhouses" to assist these unfortunate individuals, suggesting that they are undeserving of his financial aid. Though the men profess that "many would rather die" than go to the places mentioned by Scrooge, he ultimately dismisses them.

Upon Scrooge's return home, bleak imagery of his house is employed by Dickens to mirror that of his conscience. Even his meals are tainted by this grim quality: "Scrooge took his melancholy dinner in his usual melancholy tavern." Here, the repetition of "melancholy" and the **personification of his dinner** points towards the notion that every facet of Scrooge's life is permeated by **indignation.** His house is overshadowed by a literal and metaphorical darkness, remaining unlit. This is both a reflection of Scrooge's dull outlook, as well as his frugal ways despite his overwhelming wealth. After all, Scrooge comments, "darkness is cheap."

Personification: to give human-like characteristics to objects, animals or anything considered non-human.

Indignation: to feel anger or distrust due to something seeming unjust or incorrect.

Scrooge's first encounter with Marley is as an apparition on his door knocker. He promptly ignores it, although "startled" by the appearance. It is only when he hears a "clanking noise, deep down below; as if some person were dragging a heavy chain over the casks in the wine merchant's cellar," that his "colour change[s]."

Here, the "clanking" sound reflects the heavy "chains of greed" Marley's ghost is clad in, weighted with "cash-boxes, keys, padlocks, ledgers, deeds, and heavy purses wrought in steel." This list bears unmistakeable **connotations of money and wealth,** symbolising the **opportunistic pursuits Marley forged in life,** similar to Scrooge.

Sardonic: to be humorous, yet mocking or critical at the same time.

Façade: the outward appearance or something, which can often be deceptive.

Scrooge **sardonically** explains the ghost's appearance away as "an undigested bit of beef, a blot of mustard, a crumb of cheese, [or] a fragment of an underdone potato," suggesting that a stomach upset has conjured this figment of his imagination. Yet Scrooge's fear is evident. It is in this moment when Scrooge's **facade** begins to fracture in "mercy."

Marley is unperturbed by Scrooge's lack of belief, eventually prompting him to accept the apparition and ask as to why he is there. Marley laments the doom he has been bound to in the afterlife, whereby "if that spirit goes not forth in life, it is condemned to do so after death." Marley is ultimately "doomed to wander through the world" and "witness what it cannot share, but might have shared on earth, and turned to happiness." The ghost's "cry" and shaking of its chain elucidates Marley's remorse: a stark dichotomy to the sombre picture of him painted at the very beginning of the novella. The ghost warns Scrooge that his own "ponderous chain" was "as heavy and as long" as Marley's "seven Christmas Eves ago," evoking the **haunting imagery of Scrooge's literal and symbolic "chains of greed."**

The ghost laments his misunderstandings of life, and how they have led to his imprisonment in the afterlife where "regret" cannot "make amends for one life's opportunity misused." He also alludes to the "Christian spirit," in that however kindly a person might be, working for their own means will inevitably find them with insufficient "usefulness" to avoid the ghost's current fate. However, Scrooge confuses the ghost's meaning, arguing that Marley was "a good man of business." This highlights the flawed nature of Scrooge's morals. As such, the ghost retorts in agitation of the significance of "charity, mercy, forbearance, and benevolence" – a stark juxtaposition to the values fostered by Scrooge. The **metaphor** of the "dealings" of Marley's "trade" as a "drop of water in the comprehensive ocean of [his] business," **suggests the little purpose and value of pursuing a life motivated only by wealth.**

Marley concludes their interaction by warning Scrooge of the three visits he is to receive from the triad of spirits. Upon looking out of his window, Scrooge observes an "air... filled with phantoms." This **horrific and unsettling imagery** is a **momentary presage** of the afterlife that awaits Scrooge, and to which Marley's spectre belongs.

Scrooge "fell asleep upon the instant," paving the way for the three apparitions he is yet to confront.

Stave 2: The First of the Three Spirits

Summary

In stave two, Scrooge is confronted by the Ghost of Christmas Past and witnesses five key scenes. Scrooge learns that the partakers of the scenes are unable to see or hear him. Scrooge may observe only, despite his unprecedented urge to participate.

In the first scene, Scrooge is a young boy at school who remains alone – abandoned by his family and friends on Christmas Eve. The ghost remarks on the emptiness of the school, save of course for the presence of young Scrooge himself.

In the second, Scrooge is slightly older yet he remains in the same room as in the first scene. Though this time he is not alone. Rather, he is subsequently greeted by his sister Fran.

The third is a Christmas party held when Scrooge was only an apprentice. Ironically, Scrooge is found to be merry and contented, despite his contemporary hatred toward Christmas.

The fourth shows Scrooge with a woman, evidently his previous partner. The woman ultimately leaves Scrooge for his refusal to live a humble life alongside her, **foreshadowing his obsession with greed.**

The final scene witnesses this same partner as a **matron**, seated in her household with her husband and their several children. It is thus implied that whilst Scrooge descended into a life of isolation after their parting, this woman went forth into a happy marriage – the very union which Scrooge could have seized himself.

Matron: an older married woman, typically respectable and dignified.

These events from Scrooge's past frame the man he has become. It is in the second stave where Dickens compels the audience to feel some level of empathy for Scrooge.

Analysis

Scrooge awakes to the heavy "chimes of a neighbouring church" and is astounded to discover that it is midnight, despite the fact that "it was past two when he went to bed." Scrooge is **confounded** by the sequence of events which unfolded the night prior, where "Marley's Ghost bothered him exceedingly." Though he may debate whether it was "a dream or not", it is evident that Scrooge saw much truth in Marley's words.

Confounded: confused.

Bell chimes then serve as a fantastical signal of the spirits' arrivals and the intersection of the natural with the supernatural. The **onomatopoeic** repetition of the bell's "ding, dong!" is interjected with Scrooge's commentary of "a quarter past."

Onomatopoeia: a word formed from the imitation of a sound (e.g. oink, honk, hiss).

Egotistic: an excessive sense of self-importance and thinking of oneself as better than others.

This establishes a dramatic crescendo, for the reader knows that the third toll of the bell signals the arrival of the third spirit. Yet Scrooge's **egotism** has not been completely eradicated despite the previous night's events, for he "triumphantly" comments that the "hour itself" has come, yet no spirit hovers before him. However, his smugness is trumped by the "deep, dull, hollow, melancholy" sounds of the final toll, in which a "light flashed up in the room upon the instant, and the curtains of his bed were drawn." Here, the **personification** of the bell indicates the **symbolic purpose it serves in the novella.**

Hybridisation: blending two things together.

The **imagery** of the Ghost of Christmas Past's appearance is a haunting one. The narrator recounts that it was a "strange figure," much "like a child: yet not so like a child as like an old man... which gave him the appearance of having receded from the view, and being diminished to a child's proportions." This **hybridisation** of youth and age ascribes the spirit an unsettling appearance – a reflection of its supernatural duty to display past events to Scrooge. Moreover, the hair of the spirit was "white as if with age; and yet the face had not a wrinkle in it, and the tenderest bloom was on the skin." Its arms and hands are described as "very long and muscular," as though it possessed "uncommon strength." It is clad in a "tunic of the purist white" tied with a "lustrous belt, the sheen of which was beautiful." Most curiously, "a bright clear jet of light" springs from the crown of its head. The spirit is thus conveyed in a **supernatural yet angelic light.** Indeed, "white" is often associated with **purity and divinity,** whilst "light" is synonymous with **divine spirituality, and goodness.** Dickens presents the ghost as mysteriously **amorphous** and obscure, whereby "the figure fluctuated in its distinctness, painting it in an enigmatic and beguiling light." This is mirrored by its "soft and gentle" voice.

Amorphous: having no clear shape or form.

Scrooge, unsettled by the beaming light which emerges from the spirit's head, develops a "special desire to see the Spirit in his cap," and "begged him to be covered." The spirit remarks that such a cap has been made by the "passions" of those like Scrooge, forcing it to "wear it low upon... its brow." This suggests that wrongdoers like Scrooge, as literal suppressors of the spirit's beaming light, are also suppressors of all of light's connotations of goodness, kindness, and virtue.

Polysyndeton: the repetition of a conjunction (usually 'and') within a list of things.

Taking the spirit's hand, Scrooge is at once transported to a scene from Scrooge's childhood. Instantly, "a thousand thoughts, and hopes, and joys, and cares, long, long forgotten" confront him. Here, the **polysyndeton** prolongs the litany, as though it were read breathlessly by the reader. This mirrors the overwhelming reawakening of Scrooge's memories and senses, long suppressed in the hopes of numbing an entire portion of his life that he wishes to forget.

Scrooge's harsh façade further eases in this scene; the spirit comments that his "lip is trembling," and spots upon his cheek a trickling tear. Though Scrooge embarrassingly dismisses it as a "pimple," it is evident that his emotional void has been opened. Scrooge clearly remains very much attached to his past, though he has sought to neglect it, and triumphantly announces that he could walk the road "blindfold[ed]."

For the first time in the novella, Scrooge experiences an emotion beyond anger or bitterness, and is instead "rejoiced beyond all bounds" to see the other boys "in great spirits." The **personification** of the "crisp air [that] laughed to see it," mirrors the joyous nature of the scene, long foreign to Scrooge. Curiously, Scrooge is "filled with gladness" to hear the boys wishing each other Merry Christmas, though no such greeting has given him any pleasure in his adulthood.

However, the contentment of the scene is interrupted with the ghost's remark that "a solitary child, neglected by his friends, is left there" at the school. The isolated imagery of a youthful Scrooge is furthered with the image of a "lonely boy [who] was reading near a feeble fire" in a "long, bare, melancholy room." This is a **stark juxtaposition** to the group of merry boys Scrooge had just witnessed. A further foreign emotion is unearthed within Scrooge's conscience – sadness, for he "wept to see his poor forgotten self as he used to be." Here, Dickens perhaps attempts to evoke a certain level of empathy for the bitter and disgruntled old man Scrooge has become. Scrooge's earliest experiences of Christmas were clearly tainted by unwanted solitude and isolation as he was neglected by his friends and family alike.

The scene then changes once more to the same school setting, yet several years later. Scrooge however is no longer alone, greeted by his younger sister Fran who informs him that he will be going home for Christmas. Dickens provides the reader a glimpse into young Scrooge's home life, alluding to the difficulties he may have faced. Fran exclaims that "[f]ather is so much kinder than he used to be, that home's like Heaven!", suggesting that their father was an **austere** and harsh man. Ironically, this very man that young Scrooge viewed unfavourably is perhaps a reflection of elderly Scrooge himself.

Austere: someone who is strict or rigid; uncompromising.

The two siblings are taken into the schoolmaster's office, who is characterised with a "terrible voice" and a "ferocious condescension" for Scrooge. Once more, Scrooge's indignation is contextualised and somewhat validated by Dickens; his bitterness did not arise randomly, but rather, has its origins in **deep-seated experiences of shame and discontent in his youth.** In this seemingly insignificant scene, Dickens also subtly points towards the class divide between the working and middle/upper classes. Whilst Fran and Scrooge are offered a "decanter of curiously light wine" as well as "a block of curiously heavy cake," the postboy is merely offered "a glass of 'something'." Upon being presented with such a choice, the postboy declines on the basis that, "if it was the same tap as he had tasted before, he had rather not."

Greed and **frugality** are therefore, not only traits exercised by Scrooge and Marley as individuals, but by the upper classes at large. Here, Dickens perhaps **critiques broader Victorian society.** Ironically, despite Scrooge's clear affection for his late younger sister, whom he describes as a "delicate creature," he chooses to treat her only child (Bob Cratchit) with spite.

Jovial: happy, merry.

Augment: to increase in size or make larger.

The spirit and Scrooge are then transported to a different scene several years later on the busy streets of London. The pair witness the unfolding of a Christmas Eve party at the place where Scrooge was apprenticed. Dickens characterises Scrooge's boss, old Fezziwig, as a lively and **jovial** character impassioned by the celebration of Christmas. He is therefore entirely disparate to the present Scrooge. That notwithstanding, Scrooge's affection for him is clear, as he exclaims "[b]less his heart; it's Fezziwig alive again!" The narrator describes Fezziwig's voice as a "comfortable, oily, rich, fat, jovial" one. The **personification** of his voice as "oily, rich, [and] fat" associates his intonation with the hearty delicacies and meals enjoyed at Christmas time, connected with notions of warmth and comfort. Fezziwig's dialogue is permeated by enthused exclamations, **augmenting** the jolly depiction of his character.

Fezziwig insists that the apprentices cease their work at seven o'clock, and that they "have the shutters up" and clear the warehouse for a great, though humble, celebration. This can be contrasted to Scrooge's treatment of his clerk Bob Cratchit, whom he dismissed on Christmas Eve, gruffly complaining that he was to be granted the day off on Christmas Day. Scrooge, a boss himself, adopts an entirely different conduct to Fezziwig.

Ironically, the youthful Scrooge himself assists in closing up: "[t]hey charged into the street with the shutters – one, two, three – had them up in their places – four, five, six – barred them and pinned then – seven, eight, nine – and came back before you could have got to twelve, panting like race-horses." Here, the interjecting commentary of counting the seconds, increases the **accelerated rhythm** of the passage. With each counted second there is an increased anticipation and excitement. Indeed, the narrator occupies an elated tone throughout the entire scene, mirroring the good spirits of the partygoers.

Anaphora: the repetition of a particular word or phrase at the beginning of successive clauses, phrases, or sentences.

The party is frequented by a great host of guests: "[i]n came the three Miss Fezziwigs [...] In came the six young followers [...] In came all the young men and women." Here, Dickens's employment of **anaphora** mirrors the **vibrant imagery** of a strong stream of guests trickling through the doors of the warehouse. Much unlike the lonesome Christmases old Scrooge is now accustomed to, Fezziwig's Christmas is one of unity and companionship.

Dickens ascribes the scene with a profound atmosphere of nostalgia and hospitality, rendered more so with the list describing "dances, and there were forfeits, and more dances, and there was cake, and there was negus, and there was a great piece of Cold Roast, and...". Here, the **polysyndeton** prolongs the litany, augmenting the magnitude and value of each of the items, which also mirrors the breathlessness and movement of the enthusiastic dancers. However, beyond these material things, it is the dances of Mr and Mrs Fezziwig which truly enliven the party, suggesting that **emotional happiness is far more valuable than material happiness.**

Meanwhile, old Scrooge watches the scene in admiration; "[h]is heart and soul were in the scene," so much so that he forgets the ghost's presence. The ghost probes at Scrooge in false confusion: "[h]e has spent but a few pounds of your mortal money: three or four perhaps. Is that so much that he deserves this praise?" By describing money as "mortal," Dickens suggests that wealth has a temporary and curtailed quality which extinguishes quickly. It is mortal, in that it dies with the owner – as the reader will yet witness in Scrooge's voyage with the Ghost of Christmas Yet To Come, where his hypothetical death is revealed. Without hesitation, Scrooge immediately retorts, "heated by the remark, and speaking unconsciously like his former, not his latter self," that Fezziwig "[h]as the power to render us happy or unhappy; to make our service light or burdensome; a pleasure or a toil." Scrooge further asserts that Fezziwig's "power lies in words and looks... The happiness he gives, is quite as great as if it cost a fortune." The fact that Scrooge speaks in "heated" defence of Fezziwig, indicates his genuine affection towards the man, and his uncompromising willingness to counter the ghost's probing proposition that only materialism is deserving of praise. Moreover, Scrooge presents two **binaries** of human character/emotion, and materialism. He suggests that Fezziwig's "words and looks" are invaluable to the extent that you cannot "count them up" as you might with coins and pennies. Once more, Dickens emphasises the mortality of wealth.

Binaries: two opposing sets or ideas of something/two contrasting things.

Scrooge concludes that he wishes he would "be able to say a word or two to [his] clerk just now," indicating his regret of his stern treatment of Bob Cratchit, and his failure to replicate the jovial environment fostered by his previous boss, who was greatly admired by all, Scrooge very much included.

The scene then suddenly shifts once more to an exchange between Scrooge (now several years older than in the previous scene), and his fiancée. Unlike the previous scene, where young Scrooge was clearly one with the spirit of Christmas, Scrooge has changed so that there is now "an eager, greedy, restless motion in the eye." Scrooge has thus lost much of his previous fervour, and begins to eerily resemble the old and irritable Scrooge known to the reader. Evidently, concerns with **avarice** and economy have surpassed all other interests.

Avarice: to covet wealth or fortune with an uncontrollable need.

Prescient: to have knowledge of something before it happens.

The narrator **prescientl**y forewarns that these qualities presage "where the shadow of the growing tree would fall" – a haunting metaphor for Scrooge's final descent into a seemingly permanent bitterness and isolation.

Avarice: greed, materialism, selfishness.

The "fair young girl" who sits beside Scrooge, sheds "tears, which sparkled in the light that shone out of the Ghost of Christmas Past," indicating an evident rift between the couple. The girl comments that Scrooge "fear[s] the world too much," and as such, has turned to **avarice** as a remedy to his scepticism and cynicism. She laments that she has witnessed his "nobler aspirations fall off one by one, until the master-passion, Gain, engrosses" him. In other words, Scrooge has abandoned his previous attributes, giving way to greed and opportunism. The **capitalisation of the noun "Gain", personifies it,** suggesting that it is a private entity in and of itself, with its own identity and implications. It indeed reigns "master" and supreme over those who succumb to its temptations, and Scrooge is one of its many victims.

Scrooge's lover discloses that the pair had agreed to "improve [their] worldly fortune by [their] patient industry," when they "were both poor and content to be so." In other words, Scrooge had once been contended with pursuing a humble, though happy, life alongside his fiancée, but is now "another man" in his conviction on life. The scene concludes with the girl "releas[ing]" Scrooge of his partnership and loyalty to her. She realises that Scrooge is now discontent with being tied to a "dowerless girl," and so chooses to leave their relationship. Present Scrooge bemoans the "torture" the ghost has submitted him to, evidently grief-stricken at the burden of re-watching his parting scene with his lover.

Dynamism: filled with energy.

The scene shifts for the fifth and final time to reveal this same "beautiful young girl" now grown and matronly in her household, surrounded by her many children. The scene is permeated by **dynamism** and excitement, made "tumultuous" and "uproarious" by a herd of children. The "knocking at the door" signals the entrance of the woman's husband holding many Christmas presents, which the woman answers with a "laughing face and plundered dress." The scene is, in other words, the antithesis of old Scrooge's domestic reality. It represents a future which may have been available to young Scrooge had he not turned to avarice and greed in place of benevolence and humility.

The woman's husband teasingly comments that he had seen Scrooge at "his office window," where "he sat alone." He notes the rumour that "[h]is partner lies upon the point of death," obviously referring to Jacob Marley. The death of Marley thus signals Scrooge's permanent descent into isolation.

Pained by the reminder of such events, Scrooge demands that the ghost "remove [him] from this place," forcing the "extinguisher-cap" upon the ghost's head in order to be rid of it. Scrooge then falls deeply asleep, concluding his journey with the Ghost of Christmas Past.

Stave 3: The Second of the Three Spirits

Summary

In the third stave, 'The Second of the Three Spirits', Scrooge is introduced to the Ghost of Christmas Present, who differs greatly in appearance and character to the previous spirit.

The first scene unfolds on the busy streets of London, depicting the hustle and bustle of a contemporary Christmas Eve. Scrooge witnesses Christmas Eve at the Cratchit household, boasting a humble and meagre meal which the Cratchits nevertheless praise and are immensely grateful for. Scrooge himself comes into the topic of conversation, and Mrs Cratchit disparages him as selfish and unsympathetic.

Scrooge then spectates his nephew's Christmas Eve gathering, a setting so enjoyable that Scrooge begs the ghost to remain there longer. As with the Cratchits, Scrooge's name is raised with his relative, and they mock his needless greed and bitterness.

The voyage concludes with the appearance of two horrific and unsightly children who tug at the ghost's robe, the boy representing Ignorance, and the girl symbolising Want. Upon the spirits departure, Scrooge does not fall into another deep slumber, but instead, observes the Ghost of Christmas Yet To Come approaching him.

Analysis

The third stave begins with Scrooge nervously anticipating the arrival of the Ghost of Christmas Present. No longer sceptical and cynical of the spirits, Scrooge is in simultaneous awe and fear of their powers. Scrooge's own authority and composure has been reduced to that of a boy's, as like a frightened child he "established a sharp look-out all around the bed," anxiously anticipating the second spirit's arrival.

However, when the bell strikes one, the spirit has still not arrived. As such, Scrooge suspects that it may be in another room and goes to turn the lock. Ironically, in the first and second staves Scrooge was resistant to the sprits' presence, however now Scrooge willingly seeks it out himself. It is perhaps for this reason that the spirit does not immediately reveal its presence. This suggests that he has been enlightened by his own need to change his ways through his voyage with the first spirit.

The characterisation of the Ghost of Christmas Present serves as a stark contrast to that of Christmas Past. Whereas the first spirit was gentle and angelic in its appearance, the second spirit is defined by its outspokenness and gleeful nature, as well as its accompanying range of **commodities.**

Commodities: an object or product which can be purchased.

Upon entering the room, Scrooge discovers a pile of "turkeys, geese, game, poultry, brawn, great joints of meat, sucking-pigs, long wreaths of sausages, mince-pies, puddings, [...] and seething bowls of punch." The vibrant imagery of these items reflects the tangibility of Christmas and **archetypal notions of excess,** mirroring the 'present' nature of the Christmas scenes Scrooge is yet to witness. The metaphor of this pile forming a "kind of throne," associates the commodities with royalty or sovereignty, perhaps suggesting the grand scale of Christmas. The spectre itself is described as a "jolly Giant" bearing a "glowing torch." Scrooge greets the spirit "timidly [hanging] his head before" him, which reveals his departure from egotism and indignation. Indeed, he is now "not the dogged Scrooge he had been." Scrooge's inability to meet the "clear and kind" eyes of the spirit suggests his feelings of shame and embarrassment at his past selfishness. Whereas Scrooge had been sceptical and disbelieving of the spirits' existence in his interaction with the ghost of Marley, he now regards the spirit "reverently."

The narrator presents the imagery of the spirit's robe which is green with fur and quite loose, so much that "its capacious breast was bare." The spirit's feet are also described as bare, and it wears a "holly wreath" on its head. It bears "dark brown curls," a "genial face," "sparkling eye[s]," a "cheery voice," an "unconstrained demeanour" and a "joyful air." Another important description is the "antique scabbard" it wears around its waist that contains no sword. While the Ghost of Christmas Past was effeminate and cherubic, the **Ghost of Christmas Present is masculine and powerful.**

Upon informing Scrooge that the spirit is of a family of "[m]ore than eighteen hundred," Scrooge mutters that it would be a "tremendous family to provide for." Though a seemingly insignificant remark, this would suggest that Scrooge is still somewhat tied to the futile value he places upon wealth – though he has been unburdened of his previous bitterness and grimness. That notwithstanding, Scrooge is evidently willing to be morally enlightened by the spirit's teachings, for he implores the spirit to "teach" him a lesson, in hopes that he might "profit by it." He concedes that the former spirit offered "a lesson which is working now."

At once, the scene changes, and Scrooge is transported from the room in his house. He finds himself on the streets of London, confronted by the hustle and bustle of Christmas time. The paradox of the "air of cheerfulness" in the streets despite the fact that there "was nothing very cheerful in the climate or the town," elucidates the capacity of Christmas to foster values of optimism and triumph in the face of adversity – whether those adversities be trivial, like the cold weather, or more considerable, like the sickly state of Tiny Tim. This cheerful atmosphere is furthered with the imagery of people "shovelling away on the housetops [who] were jovial and full of glee," the "poulterers," "fruiterers," "jolly old gentlemen" and "shopkeepers" – amongst other city dwellers and vendors. There is a great dynamism and fast-paced nature to the scene, as though the rapid physical movement of busy city-goers were tangible to the reader. The accelerated movement of the scene is also echoed by the customers who are "hurried and so eager in the hopeful promise of the day, that they tumbled up against each other," "clashing their wicker baskets wildly" as they "r[an] back to fetch" their forgotten purchases.

The scene is **idyllic and romanticised** in its portrayal, with **quotidian** items acquiring a utopian quality. The scales on the counter do not merely ring, but make a "merry sound." The "scents of tea and coffee" are not merely fragrant, but "grateful to the nose." The raisins are not merely in abundance, but are "so plentiful and rare." The almonds are not merely pale, but "so extremely white in colour." This **hyperbolic romanticisation** continues on in the narrator's description of the cinnamon sticks, spices, candied fruit, figs, French plums, and so forth. This imagery serves to reflect the notion that all senses are heightened at Christmas, and all joys or attributes are magnified in quality. Whereas these commonplace commodities of almonds and spices may not have aroused any such awe or wonder at any other time of the year, they certainly do so at Christmas.

Quotidian: daily; everyday; normal.

In the midst of this lively scene, the spirit "shed[s] a few drops of water" from his torch on a pair of quarrellers engaged in angry words to restore their good attitude, and he "sprinkled incense" on the dinners of the poor. The scene thus remains unrivalled by the human flaw of pessimism. Scrooge inquires as to whether the spirit's "incense" would work for any diner and the spirit responds with, "[t]o a poor one most." Scrooge questions this, unable to immediately identify why a poor individual might "need[s] it most," suggesting that he is still somewhat blinded by the inflated importance he places upon economy.

Scrooge asks why the spirit would "desire to cramp these people's opportunities of innocent enjoyment" despite his great powers. The spirit responds in incredulity: "I! cried the Spirit." He thus implies that it is not the work of any supernatural or divine powers to deprive the poor of a meal. Rather, he points towards **human selfishness and greed as the root cause.** If the rich were to share their wealth with the poor, then their hardship and suffering would be tremendously diminished. Scrooge however, is blinded to this fact, as he considers the suffering of the poor to be forged in the "name" of the spirit's family. Yet the spirit debunks this presumption by observing that there are human individuals who "do their deeds of passion, pride, ill-will, hatred, envy, bigotry, and selfishness in [their] name" who claim to hold belief in the spirits' teachings, and yet are frowned upon by the spirits "as if they had never lived." In other words, the spirit suggests that there are greedy people who still parade the false façade of morality.

Scrooge and the spirit then arrive at the Cratchit household, which the spirit blesses with his torch, indicating that the poor are deserving of generosity more so than the rich. The reader is introduced to Mrs Cratchit, who is dressed poorly in a "twice-turned gown." Despite the humbleness of her gown, she still **adorns** it in ribbons "which are cheap and make for a goodly show for sixpence." This points towards her ability to make the best of her humble means. The household scene is pervaded by an air of comfort, by the smell of the goose, the "sage and onion," the fireplace and the "bubbling" of the potatoes, suggesting that wealth should not be a prerequisite for happiness.

Adorn: to decorate.

Mr Cratchit's daughter Martha, having just arrived through the door, is encouraged by the other two children to hide in an attempt to surprise their father of her presence. This childish play increases the joviality of the scene, and also expounds the narrator's assertion that "it is good to be children sometimes."

Coming home from church with Tiny Tim, Cratchit retells Tim's hope that the church-goers took note of his presence, so that they may "remember upon Christmas day, who made lame beggars walk, and blind men see." This can be seen as a **biblical allusion** to Christ's giving of miracles to the less fortunate. It points towards the admirable thanksgiving of the poor and unfortunate, and to the **theme of hope.** Tiny Tim, despite his sickliness, fosters hope and faith in the prospect of strength and recovery. This is also much like Bob Cratchit, who asserts the **alliterative idiom** that Tiny Tim is "good as gold," though, in reality, Tim's life is less than ideal. This is implicated in Cratchit's "tremulous" voice, which "trembled more when he said that Tiny Tim was growing strong and hearty," suggesting an underlying level of fearfulness. Dickens thus deplores the selfishness of the middle and upper-class who are arguably devoid of any justifiable means of complaint, much unlike the poor and less fortunate.

Idiom: a figure of speech or commonly used turn of phrase.

Despite the family's humble means, and their consequent inability to provide for a great and plentiful Christmas feast – much in contrast to the pile of gastronomic goods piled before the spirit in Scrooge's house – the family members are nevertheless appreciative of the meal prepared by Mrs Cratchit. The **free indirect speech** echoing the voice of Bob Cratchit, declares in a truncated sentence "[t]here was never such a goose," though the goose in reality is small and meagre. It is viewed through a romanticised lens by the grateful family: "[i]ts tenderness and flavour, size and cheapness, were the themes of universal admiration." Amongst the nouns "tenderness," "flavour" and "size" lies the word "cheapness," indicating the family's appreciation of the commodities within their means. Dickens induces the reader's empathy in this scene with the abject hopefulness of the Cratchits. Mrs Cratchit observes in "great delight" that the family had not finished the goose after all, referring to "one small atom of a bone upon the dish." Moreover, each family member complimented Mrs Cratchit's pudding, though "nobody said or thought it was at all a small pudding for a large family." This attitude of thanksgiving and gratitude can be contrasted to the earlier portrayal of Scrooge in the novella. Ironically, a family with little to find appreciation for exemplify the true spirit and values of Christmas, while Scrooge, a wealthy and successful individual, pessimistically bemoans the expense of paying his clerk.

Of all the members in the Cratchit family, Tiny Tim concludes their blessing of Christmas with a meaningful and genuine exclamation, "God bless us every one!" When Scrooge asks the spirit if Tiny Tim will live, it ominously replies that it sees "a vacant seat" and "a crutch without an owner." More directly, it warns that "[i]f these shadows remain unaltered by the Future, the child will die." This haunting imagery of a vacancy in the family evokes the sympathy of the reader, developing a chilled frost over the warmth of the scene just witnessed. Scrooge pleads with the ghost that Tiny Tim "be spared." In response, the ghost echoes Scrooge's previous words to the two charitable men who had entered his countinghouse seeking donations: "[i]f he be like to die, he had better do it, and decrease the surplus population." In recognition of the cruel and biting nature of his vitriol, Scrooge "hung his head to hear his own words quoted by the Spirit, and was overcome with **penitence** and grief." Where Scrooge once delivered those same words with forthright spite, devoid of any hesitation, he is now ashamed to hear them spoken by another.

Penitence: feeling remorse or regret.

The dialogue between Scrooge and the ghost is then interrupted by Bob Cratchit's sudden exclamation "I'll give you Mr Scrooge, the Founder of the Feast!" The exclamation is not a disingenuous or sarcastic one, but rather, a grateful and empathetic praise. The capitalisation of "Founder" and "Feast" elevate and champion Scrooge as though he were endowed with a formal title. Yet Bob's sympathies are not shared by Mrs Cratchit, who indignantly mocks him: "I wish I had him here. I'd give him a piece of my mind to feast upon, and I hope he'd have a good appetite for it." Despite the humble gratitude of the family, Scrooge's selfishness and frugality is so deplorable that not even he is a subject of the family's excessive appreciation. She castigates him as an "odious, stingy, hard, unfeeling man," almost as though he were stripped of his human characteristics. In this instant, the joyous spark of the scene has been suddenly diminished, like the flame of a candle; "[i]t was the first of their proceedings which had no heartiness." The narrator describes Scrooge as the "Ogre of the family," likening him to an oppressive and disfigured supernatural giant. The **metaphor** of the **"dark shadow"** cast upon the family at the mention of his name, elucidates the great power Scrooge's stinginess holds over the family, in the way it dictates their welfare. In the same way, Scrooge has equal power to endow the family with a greater level of comfort, were he more generous with Bob's salary.

The scene concludes with a final resuming of their merriment. Though they are "not well dressed," they nevertheless are "happy, grateful, [and] pleased with one another." **Dickens thus espouses the gratitude of the family as an ideal which should be fostered by the rich and poor alike on Christmas.** He suggests that it is the poor who exercise this ideal most, and the rich who are most blind to it.

Scrooge and the spirit carry on from the Cratchit family until they arrive at a household where Scrooge hears the laughter of his nephew Fred. The narrator champions laughter as a remedy to grief and woe, professing that "while there is infection in disease and sorrow, there is nothing in the world so irresistibly contagious as laughter and good-humour." The imagery of his nephew "holding his sides, rolling his head, and twisting his face into the most extravagant contortions" can be contrasted by Scrooge's characteristic bitter and indignant "[h]umbug!"

It becomes clear that the Christmas party goers are discussing their old and pessimistic relative Scrooge. Fred says he has nothing against Scrooge, suggesting simply that "his offences carry their own punishment." This assertion foreshadows Scrooge's voyage with the Ghost of Christmas Yet To Come where he discovers that this punishment must be forged in death, much like his late partner Jacob Marley – so too will Scrooge be weighted by the deplorable "chains of greed."

Astute: to clearly define or assess a situation.

Rather than castigating or condemning Scrooge, Fred merely comments that he feels "sorry for him," and that he couldn't be angry with him. This suggests that whilst Scrooge is perceived with fear and indignation by some, like the Cratchits, he is also viewed pitifully, tainted by his own flaws and misgivings. Fred **astutely** observes that Scrooge himself is the one who suffers from his own greed and bad demeanour more so than anyone else. Indeed, whilst his greed may prevent the comfort of the poor and unfortunate (like the Cratchits), Scrooge's wrongdoings are ultimately most detrimental to his own wellbeing. Scrooge, as a result, "loses some pleasant moments" and is alone, preferring to squirrel himself away in his dank office and home.

The discussion of Scrooge then ceases, and the family members go on to sing and play music. The narrator commends that "it is good to be children sometimes, and never better than at Christmas, when its mighty Founder was a child himself." This is a further **biblical allusion to the Nativity of Christ,** as well as a commentary on the importance of light-heartedness and playful joy at Christmas. Though they are adults, they play "a game at blindman's-buff" in childish merriment, much unlike Scrooge, who hides himself away in elderly disgruntlement.

Scrooge ironically, participates in a game of forfeits as well, forgetting, in his gleeful amusement, that the partakers of the scene are unable to see or hear him. Scrooge finds himself guessing the answers to the game, and pleads with the spirit to stay another "half hour." The **simile** that Scrooge "begged like a boy to be allowed to stay until the guests departed" ascribes to Scrooge a newfound playfulness and youth. Just like the playful dynamism of the guests, Scrooge too has acquired this childish **gaiety.**

Gaiety: happiness.

In the next game called "Yes and No," each player must think of an animal, whilst the other players ask questions to guess what the animal is. Fred elects Scrooge as his chosen animal, and the sister humorously guesses correctly. The party-goers then enjoy the fact that someone's guess of "is it a bear?" should have been correct. Though this commentary can be perceived as comic banter, it also indicative of the grotesque perception held of Scrooge.

Scrooge however is "imperceptibly [...] so gay and light of heart" that he is hardly offended by their shrewd humour, but instead, "would have [...] thanked them in inaudible speech." He and the spirit then make their final departure from the scene, drifting past houses and hospitals and gaols which surprisingly always had a "happy end."

Scrooge notes that since the start of their journey the spirit has aged considerably, now bearing grey hair. The ghost announces that his "life upon this Globe," being "very brief," "end to-night." As the clock strikes three quarters past eleven, Scrooge sights a "foot or a claw" protruding from the spirit's robe. The spirit then reveals them to be "two children; wretched, abject, frightful, hideous, miserable." The children "knelt down at his feet, and clung upon the outside of its garment." This **imagery** of the children is **horrific** and **unsightly, juxtaposing the traditional connotations** of sweetness and gentleness associated with children.

Dickens presents a haunting juxtaposition between the children's youth, and the ageing frailty of their appearance. They are "[y]ellow, meagre, ragged, scowling, [and] wolfish," though "graceful youth should have filled their features out and touched them with its freshest tints." Yet no such physical signs of youth are evident, instead they reach out with a "stale and shrivelled hand, like that of age." They are stripped of their human characteristics, instead compared to "monsters."

The spirit identifies the boy as Ignorance and the girl as Want. He warns Scrooge to beware of them, yet to beware the boy most of all, seeing on his "brow [...] written which is Doom."

Scrooge cries bewilderedly whether the children have "refuge or resource," yet the spirit once more uses Scrooge's own words against him, mimicking "Are there no prisons? [...] Are there no workhouses?"

Dickens ultimately employs the imagery of these two ghastly children as embodiments of the flaws which threaten the human race most. Both Want and Ignorance had afflicted Scrooge himself. It is only now, that he develops an immunity to their **beguiling** temptations. The capitalisation of Want and Ignorance serves not only to indicate these misgivings as the names of the children, but to establish them as two **personified categories applicable to the human race.**

Beguile: to enchant or entrance someone.

The third stave concludes with the disappearance of the Ghost of Christmas Present, and the nearing of a "solemn phantom, draped and hooded" which floats towards Scrooge with the **simile,** "like a mist along the ground." Scrooge remembers the prediction of Jacob Marley's ghost as the phantom approaches, foreshadowing the grim scenes Scrooge is yet to witness in the fourth stave.

Stave 4: The Last of the Spirits

Summary

Stave Four adopts a grim and bleak tone in comparison to those of the second and third staves, which establish an atmosphere of festive nostalgia, warmth, and comfort.

The stave begins with the ominous arrival of the Ghost of Christmas Yet to Come, who hovers cloaked and silent before Scrooge. It does not answer Scrooge in his questions and fears, but merely points with a "spectral hand." This newly established sinister atmosphere **presages** the scenes Scrooge is yet to witness.

Presage: to foreshadow or warn about something impending and ominous.

Scrooge, in spite of his tremulous fear of the ghost, implores it to lead him on in the hopes of learning a third and final lesson from the spirits.

The spirit takes Scrooge through a **spate** of murky and curious scenes, quite the opposite to the nostalgic and familiar scenes witnessed alongside the first two spirits. They observe a group of businessmen discussing the death of a wealthy man at the London Stock Exchange, then a group of nomads and suspect characters selling the stolen items of a dead man in a gloomy pawn shop in the slums of London, after this they witness a poor household where a husband and wife express their relief over the death of a man to whom they owed a debt, and finally they see the Cratchit family grieving over the death of their beloved Tiny Tim.

Spate: many similar scenes occurring all together, generally in quick succession.

Upon desperately pleading with the ghost to reveal the identity of the deceased man of which these Londoners speak, the ghost merely points to a freshly prepared grave, where the name Ebenezer Scrooge is inscribed on the headstone. Scrooge now understands that the spirit has shown Scrooge future scenes after his own death. He thus pledges his duty to amend his ways and honour the spirit of Christmas.

The spirit collapses and disappears, and Scrooge is returned once more to his bedpost.

Analysis

From the outset of the fourth stave, the phantom is portrayed through **grim and bleak imagery.** It approaches Scrooge "slowly, gravely, [and] silently." The movement of the phantom is more in line with the traditional notion of a ghost, as ominous and fearsome, unlike the goodwill of the first two spirits. In response to the ghost's presence Scrooge "ben[ds] down upon his knee," almost mimicking Christian **genuflection,** as though the spirit were to be revered in equal awe as Christ.

The ghost is "shrouded in a deep black garment" which obscures from sight "its head, its face, [and] its form." Nothing of the ghost's body is visible, save for "one outstretched hand." The employment of the **past participle** "shrouded" evokes the traditional notion of a shroud: a piece of cloth or sheet used to wrap a deceased person for burial. The spirit thus brings with it an air of death and mortality, a presage to the scenes Scrooge is yet to witness.

Despite his trembling fear, Scrooge implores the ghost to continue with his message in the hopes of learning the lesson the spirit is yet to teach him. He concedes that the spirit's "purpose is to do [him] good," and he accepts his presence with a "thankful heart." Scrooge it seems, has adopted a newfound capacity for gratitude, akin to the that of the Cratchits.

They enter the busy streets of London and stop beside a cluster of businessmen who are engaged in a pragmatic dialogue pertaining to the death of an unnamed man. The businessmen are all wealthy and prosperous individuals, characterised with grotesque and unsightly physical features. Perhaps Dickens intends for the physical ugliness of the men to reflect their internal deplorability. There is a "great fat man with a monstrous chin" and a "red-faced gentleman with a pendulous excrescence on the end of his nose, that shook like the gills of a turkey-cock," amongst others. Again Dickens uses simile to make comparisons between the rich, greedy men and animals, much like Scrooge's nephew did earlier in the novel, comparing him to a bear.

The businessmen however, are far from grief-stricken in their discussion of the dead man, rather, they speak with disinterest and nonchalance. One of the men continuously "yawn[s]" throughout the dialogue, suggesting a cool indifference. It is clear that the man of which they speak left no emotional impact on them in the slightest.

They do not discuss any memories of the man, nor pay their respects (as would be typically expected from acquaintances of the deceased), instead, they deliberate over what "he [has] done with his money." It is clear that the gentlemen are as much a victim of greed as the deceased.

Genuflection: to briefly kneel as a sign of reverence or respect, typically in religious worship.

Past participle: a word that can act as a verb in past tense (ending in -ed) or as an adjective.

One of the gentleman posits that the funeral is likely to be "very cheap," given he cannot think of anybody who would actually be inclined to go to it. He suggests that they organise a volunteer funeral party, in the place of grieving and willing mourners. Another gentleman coolly responds that he will consider going "if a lunch is provided." The insensitivity of the men in turn reflects the insensitivity of the deceased, who clearly left no emotive mark or made genuine connections during his life.

Another gentleman comments that he may have even been one of the deceased's "most particular friend," given they would chat every time they met. The fact that the man speaks with such irreverence is therefore indicative of the deficient ethics of both he and the deceased. All in all, it is clear that the businessmen and the deceased alike are extremely wealthy. **Dickens thus condemns the insensitivity and greed of the upper class,** suggesting that it does not deliver any meaningful prosperity either in life or in death.

Despite the fact that "Scrooge knew the men," he remains confused as to the significance of the conversation. The phantom then points to an exchange between another two businessmen, whom Scrooge also recognises. He identifies them as "very wealthy, and of great importance." It is revealed that Scrooge always attempted to maintain a good impression with these men, yet only in a "strictly [...] business point of view." There is thus an apparent emotional void in Scrooge's interactions with others. He will only accord others favourably when there is some sort of material gain to be made.

The conversation between the two men is brief, devoid of the usual **discursiveness** and animation of a typical conversation. Thus, like Scrooge's interactions, this one too is clinical and superficial in its execution; "strictly" for the sake of maintaining favourable business connections. One of the men observes that "Old Scratch has got his own at last, hey," clearly referring to the death of the man mentioned in the previous conversation Scrooge witnessed. The reader, knowing the identity of the deceased to be Scrooge himself, is invited to consider the same coldness of the men in regards to the deceased. The second man simply replies, "So I am told", and then superficially adds, "Cold, isn't it." He thus diverts the discussion from the deceased with insensitive ease. The businessmen are not mourners, but rather, indifferent observers interested only in the considerable inheritance which the deceased must have left behind.

Discursive: like a discussion, bouncing between different topics with no specific goal.

Scrooge remains confounded as to the spirit's purpose in "attach[ing] importance to conversations apparently so trivial." Indeed, in comparison to Scrooge's voyage with the previous two spirits, the scenes he is now witnessing may seem mundane and inconsequential. Scrooge concludes that the businessmen cannot be referring to his old partner Marley, for he died a long seven years ago, and it is the future which the phantom reveals. Scrooge nevertheless continues in his resolve, "feeling assured they [the conversations] must have some hidden purpose."

Scrooge is determined to absorb the significance of every scene he witnesses, most of all, when he presumably comes to view his own self. In searching through the streets for his "own image," he fails to detect his presence, and is ultimately unsuccessful. This foreshadows the knowledge which is yet to greet Scrooge: that the deceased man of which the businessmen speak is Scrooge himself.

Scrooge and the spirit then descend into a less glamorous part of London – "an obscure part of town" which is entirely foreign to Scrooge, and which he has dared not enter before. This London slum is conveyed as "foul and narrow," "the shops and houses wretched; the people half-naked, drunken, slipshod, ugly." It is penetrated by the "offences of smell, and dirt and life," and "reeked with crime, with filth, and misery." Here, Dickens employs an abundance of adjectives which all connote eeriness and poverty. The imagery of the slum illustrates a bleak and dark collection of alleys, pervaded by a foul odour and poverty-stricken Londoners. This serves as a stark contrast to the more 'civilised' streets of London known to Scrooge, which remain largely untouched by this abject poverty. ***A Christmas Carol* therefore, not only centres on the key theme of Christmas, but also alludes to the misgivings of Victorian society,** where London slums were becoming increasingly common with the new wave of city migration and industrial progress.

Scrooge and the spirit come to stop before a cheap and shady pawnshop, described as "low-browed" and "beetling" where "iron, old rags, bottles, bones and greasy offal" were found. This litany of objects infers a griminess and cheapness, dichotomising the pleasantries of plums and puddings to be found in the shopwindows of the upper-class streets of London. On the floor inside the shop, is a great pile of "rusty keys, nails, chains, hinges, files, scales, weights, and refuse iron of all kinds." Similarly, these objects also connote a **sordidness** and miscellaneous quality. This collection of metal and alloys also alludes to the increasing industrialisation of London, powered by the poor working-class. Inside the shop is an old man smoking a pipe, characterised as a "grey-haired rascal." Thus, everything to be found within the scene is presented **pejoratively,** portraying the working-class in an unglamorous and **odious** light.

Sordid: dirty or low-quality.

Pejorative: a word or sentence with negative or disparaging meaning.

Odious: gross or disgusting.

Two women, each holding a large object, and a "man in faded black" then enter the shop and are encouraged by the grey-haired man to gather in the parlour. One of the women, introduced to the reader as Mrs Dilber, defiantly asserts that "[e]very person has a right to take care of themselves. He always did." It is implicit, that the woman refers to the dead man which has become the subject of the scenes. It is also implicit, that the bundles of the women are a collection of his stolen goods.

The second woman boldly argues that they had a right to seize his belongings, given he had no heir or companion to endow them to, and so were rendered completely unowned. She suggests that the blame is to lie with the deceased himself, who willingly pursued such an isolated and independent life. She disparages the deceased as a "wicked old screw," deploring the fact that his bitterness and **indignance** prevented him from having anyone to care for him in his last hours, leaving him "lying gasping out his last there, alone by himself." This unsettling imagery clearly elucidates the isolation of the deceased, suggesting that he was alone even in his final moments of sickness and discomfort.

Indignance: anger at something that is unfair, unjust, or morally outrageous.

The woman implores the man to open the bundle so that they may each take their spoils. The group are plainly devoid of any guilt, with the woman insisting that their actions were "no sin" when the deceased was arguably a sinner in life. The man reveals an meagre collection of "a pencil-case, a pair of sleeve-buttons, and a brooch of no great value." Though the items are arguably plain and relatively inexpensive, the man, old Joe, "examined and appraised" them. When owned by a rich man, these items are relatively inconsequential. Yet when taken by the poor, they are attributed an unmatched value.

Mrs Dilber is the next member to examine her plunder. She reveals "[s]heets and towels, a little wearing apparel, two old-fashioned silver teaspoons, a pair of sugar-tongs, and a few boots." Finally, Joe inspects the second woman's spoils. First, he pulls out a pair of bed-curtains, the very ones which hung on the bed where the deceased's corpse lay. Old Joe incredulously questions the woman's bold action in taking the bed-curtains down "rings and all, with him lying there." Yet the woman remains entirely unaffected by guilt or regret, but merely comments on how the deceased does not deserve respect or reverence. Next, old Joe pulls out a blanket.

Meanwhile, Scrooge listens to the exchange in mortified horror, judging them with complete "detestation and disgust." Ironically, the reader is invited to have perceived many of Scrooge's own harsh words in a similar light in the first stave. The scene concludes with the humorous laughter of the men and women, who comically observe that the deceased "frightened every one away from him when he was alive, to profit us when he was dead." Dickens thus intimates the **futility of hoarding and needlessly shielding excessive sums of money in life,** when they ultimately **serve no useful purpose in death.** Scrooge has ultimately amassed a fortune, which is only to be exploited by a collection of poor beggars and endowed to no deserving subject.

Scrooge gradually becomes aware of the symbolic link between the deceased man of which they speak, and Scrooge himself, yet he still remains oblivious as to the true identity of the man. Instead, he merely realises that the "case of this unhappy man might be" his own, yet not that the man is in fact himself.

The scene then changes once more, to depict a corpse sheathed in cloth laying upon a bed. Dickens presents an **unsettling and disquieting personification** of the corpse: "though it was dumb, [it] announced itself in awful language." This reflects the foreboding presence the lifeless body presents. The body is ultimately "plundered and bereft, unwatched, unwept, uncared for," suggesting that even in death, he remains in a state of human abandonment.

Scrooge implores the ghost to show him a person that felt some form of emotion or affection for the deceased man, doubtfully hoping that he could not have died alone in complete neglect, unmourned by a single soul. In response, the spirit draws wide its cloak and reveals a new scene.

A mother and her children are found in their household, the mother pacing back and forth in the room, clearly waiting for the arrival of someone. Upon hearing knocking on the front door, her husband is revealed, overcome by a "serious delight of which he felt ashamed, and which he struggled to repress." At the dinner table, the woman asks him to deliver the news which he clearly bares. The woman supposes that their family is "quite ruined," yet her husband responds that there is hope, for the man of which has occupied the previous scenes is dead. The woman is immediately "thankful in her soul" at this news, and although praying for forgiveness at conjuring such a thought in response to the knowledge of someone's death, plainly recognises that gratitude and relief was the "first [...] emotion of her heart."

It becomes evident, that the 'ruin' of which the wife spoke of, is a hefty and considerable debt owed to the man who is now deceased. Ironically, the death of this man now renders the abode a "happier house," and the children are "brighter." As such, in return to Scrooge's imploration that the spirit show him "emotion caused by this man's death," the spirit is only able to display to him "one of pleasure." Any emotion of mourning or grief which Scrooge sought, is inevitably non-existent.

Scrooge then asks the ghost to show him "some tenderness connected with a death." The spirit leads him to the Cratchit household, where the family is seated around a fire. The scene is a solemn one, augmented by the simile of the "noisy little Cratchits [...] as still as statues." It becomes evident, that the family mourn the death of their beloved Tiny Tim. Bob Cratchit then enters through the door, and despite attempting to display a façade of stoicism, "[breaks] down all at once," and goes upstairs to Tiny Tim's room where his body lays.

Bob returns to his family and recounts his encounter with Scrooge's nephew Fred, who he espouses as being a benevolent and generous individual. Bob observes that he looked "just a little down." The scene concludes with the family pledging their remembrance of Tiny Tim, and his admirable character. The family's tender and grief-stricken response to Tiny Tim's death therefore, can be starkly juxtaposed with the indifferent response to the death of the unidentified man.

In this moment, Scrooge intuits that his voyage with the spectre is approaching its end, and he begs to know the identity of the man who lay dead. He also pleads, that they go to Scrooge's house, so that Scrooge may see if he has changed in the future. Yet the spectre points away in response to Scrooge's request, in the opposite direction of where Scrooge's house lies. Scrooge and the spirit enter a churchyard, ominous and unsightly with "overrun [...] grass and weeds," "vegetation's death," and "choked up with too much burying." The spirit points down to one grave in particular, ignoring Scrooge's desperate deliberation as to whether the events they have witnessed are certain, or a possibility of the future only.

In horror, Scrooge looks upon the tombstone to read his own name written there: "EBENEZER SCROOGE." Scrooge pledges to the spirit to amend his detestable ways, and to honour Christmas and the values it preaches. He promises to "live in the Past, the Present, and the Future," so that he will carry the teachings of all three spirits. He desperately pleas that he may "sponge away the writing on this stone" in a reversal of his tragic fate.

The phantom then shrivels up and disappears, and Scrooge is returned once more to the familiar normality of his bed. The stave ends here, leaving the reader wondering whether Scrooge's fate has changed for the better.

Stave 5: The End of It

Summary

Scrooge finds himself returned to his bedroom, thankful that the frightful future predicted by the third spirit has not occurred after all. Scrooge sings praise of a Merry Christmas as he frantically gets dressed. He calls out through his window to a boy walking on the street, promising to pay him half-a-crown if he hurries to the local poulterer to purchase the prize turkey hanging in the shop window. Scrooge resolves that he will send the turkey to the Cratchit household anonymously.

Upon heading out into the London streets, Scrooge apologises to one of the portly gentlemen who had sought donations for the "Poor and destitute" and promises to donate a generous sum to the cause.

Scrooge also takes up his nephew's offer to dine at his household for Christmas. The guests are shocked by Scrooge's newfound merriment and optimism.

The next morning, Scrooge arrives early at the office, with a plan to surprise Bob Cratchit. When Bob finally enters, eighteen and a half minutes late, Scrooge pretends to scold him. Midway through his false castigation however, he announces his intention to raise Bob's salary and do what he can to assist his struggling family.

The narrator concludes by revealing that Scrooge was good to his word, and continued to honour the spirit of Christmas, past, present, and future.

Analysis

The fifth stave commences with Scrooge in his bed. Upon recognising the bedpost as his own, Scrooge is flooded with immense relief, pledging to honour the teachings of the spirits past, present, and future. The first paragraph of the fifth stave is permeated by exclamations, echoing Scrooge's relieved elation.

The narrator reveals that Scrooge's face is "wet with tears," for he "had been sobbing violently" in his voyage with the third spirit. Unlike the first stave, where Scrooge was presented as entirely insensitive and emotionless, he is now overcome with emotion.

Scrooge frantically begins to get dressed, turning his garments "inside out, putting them on upside down, tearing them, mislaying them." In excited helplessness Scrooge exclaims, "I don't know what to do!" The fact that he is "laughing and crying in the same breath," reveals his newfound capacity for feeling and emotion.

He relays a spate of similes: "I am as light as a feather, I am as happy as an angel, I am as merry as a schoolboy. I am as giddy as a drunken man." These are all things which Scrooge would have indignantly attributed as a "humbug" only four staves earlier.

Scrooge laughs amidst his restless glee. The narrator posits that "for a man who had been out of practice [...] it was a splendid laugh, a most illustrious laugh." Here, glee seems almost native to Scrooge, as though it were embedded within his conscious merely waiting to be unearthed.

Scrooge compares himself to a baby, thus associating himself with rebirth and renewal. Like a mere child, Scrooge must relearn the most basic of moral lessons and the most human of instincts. This is his chance to discard his old ways, and restart his life afresh with a clean conscience.

The church bells sound in the background with the **repeated exclamatory onomatopoeia,** "[c]lash, clang, hammer; ding, dong, bell!" Where the sounding of the bell had previously signalled uncertainty and fear in his interactions with the three spirits, they now echo happiness and merriment.

The weather too, is pleasant and joyous. Devoid of "fog" and "mist," it is "clear, bright, jovial, [and] stirring" with "[g]olden sunlight," the **pathetic fallacy** of which reflects Scrooge's optimism.

Pathetic fallacy: to assign human emotions to a non-human object.

Scrooge then calls down to a nearby boy on the street through his window, asking what day it is. The boy, of course, replies that it is Christmas Day. Scrooge asks the boy to purchase the prize turkey hanging in the shop window of the local poulterer, offering to pay him half-a-crown in recompense if he runs there and back within five minutes. The boy is off in a shot, meanwhile Scrooge gleefully resolves to send the turkey anonymously to the Cratchit household.

When the turkey arrives at Scrooge's door, it is so large that Scrooge orders a cab for it to be delivered to the Cratchit household. This passage is dominated by **anaphora:** "[t]he chuckle with which he said this, and the chuckle with which he paid for the Turkey, and the chuckle with which he paid for the cab, and the chuckle with which he recompensed the boy, were only to be exceeded by the chuckle with which he sat down breathless in his chair again, and chuckled till he cried." Here, the **repetition** of chuckling elucidates the contentment and delight which now permeates Scrooge's conduct. This is reflected in the unsteadiness of his actions. The "hand in which he wrote the address" to send the turkey to the Cratchits is a shaky one, whilst shaving also was difficult. Scrooge dances as he shaves, and would have been satisfied even if "he had cut the end of his nose off." **Events are now viewed by Scrooge through an innately optimistic lens.**

Scrooge then dresses himself in his best clothes, prepared to enter out into the merry streets of London. There are people bustling up and down the streets just as he had seen in the vision with the Ghost of Christmas Present. As he walks, he greets everyone with a "delighted smile," and looks "so irresistibly pleasant" that fellow Londoners greet him with a Merry Christmas. Where such a cheerful greeting had previously angered Scrooge, and propelled him to respond with a disgruntled "humbug!", Scrooge now considers them to be the **"blithest** [words] in his ears."

Blithe: happy; cheery.

As Scrooge continues, he spots in the near distance one of the portly gentleman who had entered his counting-house only one day prior, seeking donations for the less fortunate people of London. As Scrooge observes him, there is a "pang across his heart" to consider what the gentleman must think of him and his greedy frugality. Despite his shame however, Scrooge pursues the path in front of him, determined to confront the gentleman. Not only does Scrooge approach him at leisure, but he is "quickening his pace," suggesting his eagerness to make amends and redeem his previous snobbery. Scrooge greets the gentleman with a cheerful Merry Christmas, and offers his sincere hope that he was successful in garnering donations the day prior.

The gentleman responds in confused bewilderment to Scrooge's changed character, posing "Mr Scrooge?" Scrooge responds by pleading for the man's forgiveness, and whispers in his ear his intention to donate a considerable some to the "Poor and destitute." Though the specific sum is not disclosed to the reader, its generosity is clear, for the man responds in speechless elation and astonishment. Scrooge concludes the encounter by profusely thanking him, though it is Scrooge who has done the gentleman a favour.

Scrooge then heads to the local church, watching the busy hustle and bustle of the London streets, patting children on the head, interacting with beggars, and observing kitchens through the windows of houses.

The narrator recounts that "everything could yield him pleasure." He thus, is now able to seek enjoyment in the diurnal and quotidian qualities of life, whereas in the past, only the **scintillating** shimmer of coins could have aroused equal satisfaction.

Scintillating: shiny and attractive.

In the afternoon, Scrooge then walks towards the house of his nephew Fred. His anxiousness is conveyed by the way in which he "passed the door a dozen times." When he develops the "courage to go up and knock," the door is opened by a girl who leads Scrooge to the dining room where Fred and his wife are present.

Fred greets Scrooge with elated surprise, so much so that he nearly "shake[s] his arm off." Scrooge is instantly welcomed by the family, feeling "at home in five minutes." The guests slowly arrive just as he saw them in his vision with the Ghost of Christmas Present. Here, the **exclamatory anaphora** elucidates the successful merriment of the Christmas party: "Wonderful party, wonderful games, wonderful unanimity, won-der-ful happiness!" The narrator adopts the **free indirect speech of Scrooge himself,** as though he were shouting these words in overwhelming glee.

Scrooge heads to his office early the next morning, with a plan in mind to surprise his poor clerk Bob Cratchit. Just as Scrooge had anticipated, Bob arrives a "full eighteen minutes and a half" late. Bob rapidly removes his hat and comforter, and heads quickly to his stool, immediately writing away with his pen in a desperate and fearful attempt to make up for lost time. Scrooge then feigns anger, growling a disgruntled hello, asking "[w]hat do you mean by coming here at this time of day?" Bob responds by profusely apologising. Scrooge replies that he refuses to "stand this sort of thing any longer," as though he were about to fire Bob. Yet, at that moment, he drops his pretence and announces his intention to raise Bob's salary. Scrooge wishes Bob a Merry Christmas, and pledges to assist and support Bob's family.

Scrooge proves to uphold his word, doing all he had promised and much more. Tiny Tim does not perish, and instead Scrooge becomes a "second father" to him. He becomes a good friend and businessman, an entirely changed man from what he was. Scrooge ignores the perplexed laughter at those around him who recognise the change in him, satisfied with the fact that his "own heart laughed."

Scrooge is not visited again by any of the three spirits, but rather, lives by the "Abstinence Principle" from this point forth, meaning that the spirits' teachings are not required due to his newfound reformation. Scrooge is able to keep the morals and values of the Christmas sprits alive within him for the rest of his life. The novella concludes with the earnest words of Tiny Tim: "God Bless Us, Every One!" The narrator thus invites the reader to go forth with these same new principles learnt by Scrooge, establishing the moral teaching of Christmas as a universal one.

Section 4

Character Analysis

Ebenezer Scrooge

Ebenezer Scrooge is the protagonist of Charles Dickens' novella *A Christmas Carol,* and is **depicted as a bitter an unpleasant man** who views Christmas as a "humbug!" It is clear that he is solely concerned with wealth and financial gain, paying his poor clerk Bob Cratchit a meagre wage, and refusing to donate to or help others in any way.

Due to Scrooge's rejection of everyone who enters his life, most notably his nephew Fred, Scrooge is a highly isolated character. Despite his blatant greed and ignorance, the reader cannot help but pity him for his chilling solitude. Scrooge's indignant outlook on life however, transforms with the visits of the three spirits. Thus, the Scrooge we see in the last stave of the novella is entirely different from that witnessed in the first stave. By the end of the novella, Scrooge is depicted as a generous, charitable, and benevolent character. He has changed his ways, and pledges to honour Christmas and all that it represents.

Scrooge's character is used by Dickens to **represent the broader issues in Victorian society** – specifically greed, want, ignorance, and indifference to the poor. Through Scrooge, Dickens thus imparts his core message – that greed and individualism can only lead to an isolating and sad life, and to achieve true happiness one must be compassionate and kindhearted to people from all walks of life.

The Ghost of Christmas Past

The Ghost of Christmas Past is the first of the three spirits to greet Scrooge. The spirit is characterised with a peculiar and obscure appearance. It seems to possess several characteristics of an elderly individual, yet nevertheless simultaneously has a youthful appearance. This **reflects the elusive notion of time,** and the **intrinsic link between the past, present, and future.** Most notably, the spirit has a beam of light which shoots from its head, only able to be extinguished by a cap which it carries with it. This light, and the white of its tunic, characterise the spirit as angelic or spiritual, connoting purity and divinity.

This spirit's role in the novel is to show Scrooge several scenes from his past which contribute to his character development. These scenes elucidate Scrooge's difficult and lonely past, and outline his descent into greed, thus playing into the theme of time in the novel.

The Ghost of Christmas Past imparts the perils of greed and the merits of embracing the Christmas spirit to Scrooge, and help him come to the realisation that while wealth may offer material gains, it also ultimately cannot provide any of the fundamental aspects of human relationships and empathy.

The Ghost of Christmas Present

The Ghost of Christmas Present shows Scrooge various scenes from the present, including Christmas dinner at the Cratchit household and the Christmas celebration hosted by Scrooge's nephew Fred.

The second spirit is very different in appearance from that of the first. It wears a long robe, carries a torch, and is found beside a great pile of Christmas food and commodities. This spirit is portrayed as much more masculine than the previous spirit, which had an almost cherubic presence. The spirit is also characterised quite jovially, with "a genial face" and a "jovial air." This is solidified in his duty in the novel: to show Scrooge the present, which entails the fun and joyful Christmas celebrations occurring across London – everything Scrooge is missing out on.

In his second voyage, Scrooge, above all, is invited to contrast his own obsession with wealth and prosperity, with the humility and gratitude of the Cratchits. They do not require material means to fulfil their enjoyment of Christmas, Scrooge thus recognises the pitfalls of greed, and the need for generosity.

Moreover, through the scenes The Ghost of Christmas Present takes him through, Scrooge realises his desire for human companionship. The spirit imparts the knowledge that Scrooge's isolation and solitude ultimately serve him no valuable purpose, and instead have caused him to further fall into the pit of avarice.

The warped and disfigured children which appear from the spirit's robe are also of great significance. Each child, symbolising Want and Ignorance respectively, point towards the great flaws of Victorian society – and all societies at large.

The Ghost of Christmas Yet to Come

The Ghost of Christmas Yet to Come is the most elusive and mysterious of all. It is cloaked in robes, has an indecipherable figure, and does not speak verbally to Scrooge. Instead, it merely points with its "spectral hand."

Unlike the visits of the first two spirits – which largely evoked positive emotions for Scrooge, and were merry in their depictions – the scenes unveiled by the third ghost are bleak and melancholy.

The spirit reveals Scrooge's hypothetical death – should he not change in character – and shows him that the responses of Londoners to his passing are less than empathetic. Not a single individual mourns or grieves for Scrooge. Instead, they treat his death with indifference. The only emotion produced from his death is ultimately one of happiness, demonstrated by the relief of two who are indebted to Scrooge.

Scrooge learns the futility of greed when all it produces is isolation, abandonment, and neglect. The money he has so desperately hoarded in life ultimately serves him no purpose in death. Dickens thus warns against the perils of materialism, and the consequences of unchecked avarice. Scrooge, horrified by the visions he sees, pledges to change his ways to avoid his abominable fate.

Jacob Marley

Jacob Marley was Scrooge's former business partner. They had founded their firm, named Scrooge and Marley, together many years ago. Although Marley has been dead for seven years prior to the commencement of the novella, it is implicit that Marley was equal to Scrooge in greed and avarice.

The death of Marley ultimately marked Scrooge's descent into his complete isolation. Though Scrooge did not necessarily view Marley as a companion, he held him in high regard as an **illustrious** business partner.

Illustrious: greatly successful.

Marley regains his presence in Scrooge's life with his appearance to him as a ghost. Marley is weighted in heavy chains when he appears to Scrooge, and is in an unsightly and terrifying form. Marley calls them the "chains of greed," warning Scrooge that he too will bear this "ponderous chain" if he does not amend the ills he has caused in life. Initially, Scrooge remains somewhat unconvinced by Marley's warning of the visits of the three spirits, even attempting to test the ghost's authenticity.

However, by the end of the novella, Scrooge is thankful of Marley's appearance, and views the knocker on his door – which had taken the shape of Marley's face – with profound appreciation and gratitude. Through changing his ways, Scrooge avoids the miserable fate which had befallen his partner.

Bob Cratchit

Bob Cratchit is Scrooge's poor clerk who works in his countinghouse. Scrooge pays Bob poorly and treats him as a lowly subordinate. It is clear that Bob is fearful of his boss and attempts to avoid confrontation.

In Scrooge's voyage with the Ghost of Christmas Present, Scrooge's familial situation is revealed. It is evident that Bob comes from a very poor family, and has a sickly child, Tiny Tim. Despite their humble means, the family nevertheless make the most of what is available to them, and are satisfied in the happiness and joy that they bring each other.

By the end of the novella, Scrooge pledges to amend his selfish ways, and to aid the Cratchit household in any way he can: both financially and emotionally. Scrooge becomes a "second father" to Tiny Tim, and assists in avoiding his tragic death predicted by the Ghost of Christmas Present.

Fred

Fred is Scrooge's nephew. He is initially introduced to the reader when he enters Scrooge's countinghouse. Though Scrooge treats him with bitterness and dislike, Fred is nevertheless fond of his uncle, not taking his criticisms and complaints to heart. Whilst Scrooge declares that Christmas is a "humbug," Fred views it in an entirely positive light, **exalting** the generosity and integrity it evokes.

Exalting: supporting; championing.

In the vision displayed by the Ghost of Christmas Present, Fred echoes his pity for his uncle, focusing more on his isolation and solitude, rather than his malice and misdeeds.

As such, Fred openly welcomes his uncle at the conclusion of the novella when Scrooge visits his household for Christmas dinner. Fred represents the true meaning of Christmas, and the way in which it should be carried out and executed by others. Thus, Fred acts as a character foil to Scrooge, allowing readers to contrast the two views on Christmas and see Scrooge's true nature as a bitter and caustic man.

Tiny Tim

Tiny Tim is the sickly, though beloved, child of Bob Cratchit. It is clear that his family is incredibly devoted to him, and endeavour to aid and protect him in any way possible.

Though Tiny Tim is evidently weakened and unwell, he nevertheless pursues his life in a light of positivity and gratitude. One of the most renowned quotes from Charles Dickens' novella *A Christmas Carol,* is the exclamation "God bless us, every one!" These are the words spoken by Tiny Tim at Christmas dinner, and he echoes them with the most gratitude and genuineness of all of his family members.

Dickens thus creates Tiny Tim to be the **idealistic embodiment** of thanksgiving, appreciation, and optimism at Christmas time. Ironically, although Tiny Tim is the weakest of all of his family members, he is also the most grateful. Tiny Tim's hypothetical death thus also represents the death of the Christmas spirit that he embodies.

It is Scrooge's intervention which saves Tiny Tim's life and preserves his message of Christmas cheer. The novella concludes with Tiny Tim's very words, "God bless us, every one!", and therefore can be taken as one of the most central messages of the entire novella.

The portly gentlemen

Two portly gentleman enter Scrooge's counting-house on the morning of Christmas Eve, seeking donations for the "Poor and destitute" of London. Due to Scrooge's renowned wealth, the gentlemen assume that Scrooge will donate a sum of some sort. However, Scrooge staunchly declines, selfishly pointing towards "prisons" and other established institutions as suitable means of support.

However, in the fifth stave, Scrooge retracts his previous words, and openly chooses to donate a generous sum to the foundation, astounding the gentleman with his newfound charity. The dialogue of the gentlemen highlights the great magnitude of suffering and poverty at Christmas time, much in contrast to the merriness of the middle and upper-classes. In this way, Dickens seeks to establish a critique of Victorian society and the stark class divide between the rich and poor. Dickens perhaps suggests that this divide should be bridged with the generosity of the more fortunate.

Fezziwig

Fezziwig is Scrooge's former boss from when he was apprenticed as a young adult. Fezziwig is first introduced to the reader in the vision of the Ghost of Christmas Past, where the spirit depicts the Christmas party he hosted.

Though the party is a relatively humble one and entailed no great expense on Fezziwig's behalf, it is greatly treasured by the guests due to the optimism and merriment of his character. Scrooge comprehends that it is Fezziwig's vibrant nature which is so lauded by the guests, rather than any material pleasures he provides.

Like Fred and Tiny Tim, Fezziwig becomes the embodiment of how Christmas should be celebrated and viewed by individuals.

Belle

Belle is Scrooge's former fiancée. She is introduced to the reader in the vision displayed by the Ghost of Christmas Past.

Belle ultimately left Scrooge due to his developing traits of greed and avarice, which had replaced his previous humility and generosity. Belle comments on Scrooge's changed nature, and her inability to live alongside someone who will never be satisfied by non-material gains.

Belle ultimately marries another man, and fosters a large and happy family. Much unlike Scrooge who festers in isolation, Belle has established a joyful and fulfilling life.

Fran

Fran is Scrooge's younger sister, who is introduced to the reader in the vision presented by the Ghost of Christmas Past.

Fran comes to retrieve Scrooge from his school, so that they may return home for Christmas. Fran is depicted as a gleeful and delightful child, made merry by the excitement of Christmas and the companionship of her brother. Ironically, though Scrooge displays clear affection for his late sister, he chooses to treat her only son with cruel indifference.

Fran, like Fred, Fezziwig, and Tiny Tim, honours the spirit of Christmas.

Section 5

Key Themes Analysis

Christmas

Charles Dickens's novella is essentially a **Christmas story** and **Christian allegory,** which advocates a moral lesson both to a highly conservative and religious Victorian society and modern audiences alike.

Dickens divides his novella into five staves as opposed to five chapters, mimicking the basic structure of a song or carol, defined by a beginning, middle, and end. As such, by establishing a parallel between his novella and a Christmas carol, Dickens evokes the joyful and merry connotations of Christmas.

Dickens ascribes Christmas time a joyous and magical quality through his vivid imagery of the streets of London which surround Scrooge's firm. In his voyage with the Ghost of Christmas Present, the "people who were shovelling away on the housetops were jovial and full of glee," and even "the scales descending on the counter made a merry sound." Thus, Christmas takes on a fantastical quality. It is this nature of jubilation and thanksgiving which Scrooge must learn in his lesson with the three spirits. This 'Christmas spirit' is epitomised by the characters of Bob Cratchit, Scrooge's nephew Fred, and Tiny Tim.

However, Dickens also uses Christmas as a means of pitifully dichotomising the struggle of the London poor. Christmas, typically, is a time of indulgence, characterised by the "[h]olly, mistletoe, red berries ivy, turkeys, geese, game, poultry, bran, meat, pigs, sausages, oysters, pies, puddings, fruit, and punch" piled before the Ghost of Christmas Present. This notion of excess is to be juxtaposed by the meagre indulgences available to the Cratchits, namely a feeble turkey and small pudding.

Moreover, the biting nature of winter's cold also serves to reflect the struggles and difficulties of London's poor. This bleak and harsh weather ultimately exacerbates the difficulties faced by those in poverty.

Thus, Dickens presents the Christmas spirit as a Christian ideal, while simultaneously using Christmas indulgence as a means of contrasting the difficulties of the poor in the Victorian era.

Compassion and forgiveness

In *A Christmas Carol*, Charles Dickens espouses **compassion as the key antidote to greed and ignorance.** Whilst characters like Fred, Bob Cratchit, and Tiny Tim are defined by their limitless ability to empathise with others, Scrooge is deficient in this quality.

Despite the hardships Scrooge's greedy frugality has inflicted upon the Cratchit family, Bob Cratchit nevertheless attempts to silence his wife when she begins to castigate Scrooge's lack of generosity at the dinner table on Christmas.

Rather, Cratchit champions Scrooge as the "Founder of the Feast," and is grateful for his pay despite the bitter conditions Scrooge subjects him to.

Likewise, Fred is also compassionate towards his uncle. He invites Scrooge to dine with his family on Christmas, and ultimately pities rather than despises Scrooge. He considers Scrooge to be lonely and insular at his own expense. When Scrooge appears at his doorstep on Christmas Day, Fred instantly greets him with delight rather than indignance.

By stark contrast, **Scrooge is unable to sympathise with others,** above all, those who are less fortunate than he. It is this uncompassionate nature which the spirits seek to remedy in the visions they portray to Scrooge. In the first stave, Scrooge bitterly refuses to donate any funds to London's poor, turning the gentlemen away in anger. He selfishly suggests that the poor should rely on the London prisons and union houses, and in their absence, should willingly confront their own death.

Scrooge is also acutely unsympathetic towards Bob Cratchit and his family. He continues to pay Bob a low wage and subject him to meagre conditions, though he is aware of the struggles of his family – particularly Tiny Tim.

Dickens thus espouses Scrooge's newfound compassion after his exchanges with the spirits, as the epitome of Christmas' central message. No longer is he unfeeling and insensitive. Instead, he purchases and sends the prize turkey to the Cratchit household anonymously, and offers a generous donation to the London's poor.

Family

Dickens posits that family is the central root of Christian Christmas ideals. The characters of Bob Cratchit, Fezziwig, Scrooge's ex-fiancée Belle, and Fred can be said to epitomise this ideal of the **united and harmonious familial structure.**

Despite their humble means and financial struggle, the Cratchit household present as a strong, united front, supported by their appreciation of each other, even if they are not supported financially. Their love for Tiny Tim epitomises this family cohesion. Though they are dressed shabbily and are stripped of any indulgences, they are nevertheless able to find contentment and merriment in their own company.

Likewise Fezziwig, Scrooge's old boss, also embodies these family values. In the second stave, Fezziwig is able to light up the room with his glowing optimism, and he and his wife farewell each of their Christmas party guests as they leave. Though the party that he hosts is not an expensive one, Fezziwig's charisma nevertheless renders it priceless.

Moreover, Scrooge's former fiancée ultimately chooses to leave him because of his changed nature and newfound greed and opportunism. She recognises that he is now unwilling to pursue a humble life as a father. Whilst Scrooge festers in an unfulfilling life of loneliness, Belle goes on to marry and raise a happy and joyous family.

Fred, Scrooge's nephew, implores Scrooge to be an involved member of their family, though Scrooge presents no interest. Fred's forgiveness of Scrooge's unsympathetic ways represents all that family should embody: **compassion towards all family members.**

With the teachings of the three spirits, Scrooge inevitably learns this moral lesson, reacquainting himself with his forgiving nephew, and becoming a "second father" to Tiny Tim.

Greed and generosity

Greed and generosity are essentially **antonyms.** Whilst greed implies opportunism, selfishness, and frugality, generosity suggests compassion, empathy, and selflessness. These two opposing words can be linked under the same theme since Scrooge follows a trajectory from one to the other.

Antonym: words which have opposite meanings.

In the first stave, Scrooge is introduced to the reader as the epitome of avarice and **cupidity.** Yet, by stark contrast, in the fifth stave Scrooge is newly defined by his bounty and sympathy, no longer privy to holding on to each and every penny.

Cupidity: the want for money and possessions.

In the first stave, it becomes clear that Scrooge's sole interest lies in his business affairs. Even at the death of his long-term business partner Jacob Marley, Scrooge wasn't grieved about the loss of Marley himself, but more so about the fact that he was such a successful and prosperous businessman.

Scrooge ultimately denies the portly gentlemen a donation to their funds for the London's poor, and he provides Bob Cratchit with a meagre salary and humble work conditions, despite the struggling and poverty-stricken nature of his family. Scrooge feels no remorse for his actions, but rather, is satisfied with his infinite ability to conserve his money and avoid unnecessary costs.

It is through the lessons of the spirits that Scrooge's greed gradually dissipates as he acquires a newfound sense of compassion. Upon re-witnessing Belle's neglect of him, and spectating Christmas dinner at the Cratchit household, Scrooge recognises the futility of greed and obscene wealth.

It is because of Scrooge's acquisition of generosity that he avoids the "chains of greed" which bind the Ghost of Jacob Marley, confining and constraining him indefinitely in the cruel afterlife.

By the fifth stave, Scrooge willingly shares his wealth for the good of his London comrades, sending for the prize turkey at the local poulterer which is "twice the size of Tiny Tim," and donating a large some to London's poor. He does what he can to assist the Cratchit family, raising Bob's salary and becoming a "second father" to Tiny Tim.

As such, Dickens suggests that generosity is the antidote to greed and a prerequisite for a just and harmonious society.

Isolation

In *A Christmas Carol*, Scrooge is an acutely isolated character. This isolation is **partly self-inflicted** through his own greed and oppression of others. However, Scrooge's voyage with the Ghost of Christmas Past also unveils the isolating nature of Scrooge's childhood, which may have **subconsciously planted the seeds of bitterness and indignation.**

The death of Scrooge's business partner Jacob Marley firmly marked his descent into complete solitude. Though Scrooge had viewed his friendship with Marley in a strictly business sense only, he nevertheless served as a companion. This is intimated by Belle's husband in the second stave, who describes Scrooge as "quite alone in the world."

Scrooge however, has also willingly placed himself in this position of loneliness, shunning anyone who threatens to intervene in his path of efficient opportunism and money making. In the first stave, Scrooge turns away all manner of potential companions: his nephew Fred, his clerk Bob, the portly gentlemen, and the boy who stops by Scrooge's door in hopes of singing a Christmas carol.

In the third stave, Scrooge's nephew astutely observes that Scrooge's greed and bitterness has ultimately done nothing but render him isolated, and has preventing him from forging any valuable connections with friends and family alike. It was this very greed which propelled his former fiancée to leave him.

Even the working class thieves at the pawnshop in the fifth stave note Scrooge's isolation, observing that he ultimately died alone. Indeed, Scrooge's death does not stir any grief or mourning. In fact, the only emotion bought about by his death is one of happiness, encapsulated by the thankful relief of the husband and wife who had owed Scrooge a debt.

The scenes revealed in the second stave however by the Ghost of Christmas Past, also point towards the chilling and unwanted isolation of Scrooge's childhood. Scrooge and the spirit ultimately witness him as a young boy all alone at school, in stark juxtaposition to the other boys they had witnessed playing about in merry enjoyment. Dickens also alludes to the strict and austere nature of Scrooge's father, which fostered an isolating boyhood.

As such, Scrooge is **both a victim of isolation and a perpetuator of it.** Regardless, Dickens presents isolation as a dangerous state to be avoided, championing companionship and friendship in its place.

Social inequity: Victorian society

Although *A Christmas Carol* presents as a **universal tale for historical and modern audiences alike,** Dickens makes a pointed critique of his contemporary Victorian society in particular (see page 4 for a more detailed overview of the Victorian era). Dickens essentially condemns the strong class divides within British society, and the exploitation of the working-class by the wealthy. We see this exploitation on a more personal scale between Scrooge and his poor clerk Bob Cratchit.

In *A Christmas Carol,* most characters can be identified by the class they belong to. In other words, the reader is conscious of who is poor and who is rich. The result is two binaries of social classes divided by a great chasm of inequality.

In Scrooge's voyage with the Ghost of Christmas Past, Dickens's description of the setting makes the social status of the area in which the pawnshop is found evident, though Dickens never actually uses the term 'working class'. The London slum is described as "foul and narrow; the shops and houses wretched; the people half-naked, drunken, slipshod, ugly." Dickens does not actually have to spell out in black and white that this part of London is an acutely poor one, rather, this is conveyed through his **pejorative language.** This can be contrasted to the abundance of plums, puddings, and spices to be found in the shop windows where Scrooge lives.

Dickens condemns the ignorance and greed of the rich in respect of the poor through the character of Scrooge. From the outset of the novella, Scrooge's selfish frugality is made very clear. He is harsh with his poor clerk Bob Cratchit, paying him a meagre salary and reluctantly granting him the day off on Christmas Day. He is likewise bitter with the portly gentlemen and refuses to offer a donation to him. Despite Scrooge's immense wealth, and his clear ability to aid those less fortunate than he is, he refuses to do so due to his own egotism.

It is Scrooge's voyage with the Ghost of Christmas Present, which largely remedies his greed. Observing the joy and contentment of the Cratchit household in spite of their meagre celebration, Scrooge recognises that happiness is not synonymous with wealth. The spirit ultimately asserts that it is those driven by "pride, ill-will, hatred, envy, bigotry, and selfishness" who perpetuate the suffering of the poor, rather than any higher or divine power. When the two deformed and unsightly children emerge from the spirit's robe, it warns Scrooge to beware them both (Want and Ignorance), yet he warns against Ignorance most of all. This suggests that ignorance, and therefore an inability to empathise with the less fortunate, is one of the root causes of the struggle of the poor.

Scrooge's newfound generosity by the end of the novella is thus championed by Dickens as the solution to the greed of the rich and the suffering of the poor in the Victorian era. **With altruism, the gulf between the rich and poor need not be so great.**

Time: past, present, and future

In *A Christmas Carol,* the different facets of time – past, present, and future – are symbolised by the Ghost of Christmas Past, the Ghost of Christmas Present, and the Ghost of Christmas Yet to Come respectively. Time is depicted as something which shapes and influences humans: individuals are informed by their past experiences, which influence their present actions, and therefore determine their futures. One of the **central messages of the novella is perhaps that a favourable fate comes from favourable actions.** That is, by acting with benevolence, one's future is also likely to reflect this kindliness. In contrast, by acting selfishly, only negative consequences can ensue.

In each of his voyages with the three spirits, Scrooge acquires a different and valuable lesson. In his journey with the first spirit, we learn of Scrooge's childhood – a boy who lived an isolating and unloved life under his father. It is through these scenes that the audience begins to understand why Scrooge may have become the rancorous and solitary character he is in the present day. So time, and the interaction of past, present, and future, is then seen as a predictor of a person's outcomes in life, with the spirits using it as a powerful motivator to profess values of goodness, kindness, and joy. The Spirit of Christmas Past takes Scrooge into his previous years where he learns that happiness lies not in wealth and riches, but in less tangible ideals like companionship and gratitude. Fezziwig for instance, throws a merry yet humble Christmas party. Though he has not made any great expenses on the celebration, he is championed by the party-goers nonetheless. Scrooge recognises that it is Fezziwig's spirit and optimism which makes the party enjoyable, rather than any material qualities. Moreover, Scrooge's former fiancée ultimately leaves him due to his increasing greed and apathy. While Scrooge pursues a lonely and isolating life of wealth, Belle pursues a humbler life of happiness married with children. Scrooge's choice, though a more lucrative one, did not actually acquire him contentment. Thus, the lesson Scrooge (and we) should learn when looking to the past is that sometimes we pursue ephemeral and selfish short-term happiness that we will come to regret later.

In his journey with the second spirit, Scrooge learns the dangerous temptations of Want and Ignorance. Scrooge recognises that greedy ambition ultimately leads to isolation and unwelcomed solitude, just as he finds himself somewhat estranged from Fred and his family. Likewise, Ignorance prevents individuals from empathising with others, further perpetuating greed and apathy. Scrooge's insensitivity towards the poor ultimately stems from his inability to truly comprehend their struggles beyond a superficial level. It is here, in the present, that we learn the outcomes of Scrooge's decisions in the past. His developing greed and avarice, and consequential split from his fiancée has led him to shun all affection in the present, leaving him to only have ghostly interactions at Fred's party, and be unable to alter Tiny Tim's fate. The second spirit, and the terrifying creatures Ignorance and Want, thus impart the message that greed and the inability to empathise with the poor both stem from past decisions, and affect relationships in the present, leaving one alone and pleading for the company of others.

Scrooge's final journey with the third spirit teaches him the futility of wealth when all it yields is isolation. Scrooge learns that not one soul is truly grieved by his death; the only emotion produced from it is in fact one of happy relief. This is to be contrasted with the death of Tiny Tim, which causes great grief and mourning within the Cratchit household. This not only sums up Scrooge's journey, but also impresses the point that **time is something which shapes an individual and determines their fate.** However it is also deemed as something that can be altered depending on the actions a person will take in the present to change their future and avoid repeating the past.

Ultimately, through Scrooge's interactions with the less fortunate, Dickens condemns the greed of the rich and the subsequent suffering of the poor. He thus invites his Victorian reader to embrace the true spirit of Christmas, and acquire an outlook of generosity rather than self-importance by offering the idea that **no matter what someone has done in the past, they can change the present if they shun the sins of ignorance and want and invite compassion and goodwill.**

Section 6

Structural Features Analysis

Symbolism

Symbolism is employed liberally throughout *A Christmas Carol* as a means of elucidating key themes and ideas which are central to the text. Some of the most important symbols include Jacob Marley's chains, the three spirits, the two children of the Ghost of Christmas Present, food, light, the weather, and church bells.

Jacob Marley's chains

The Ghost of Jacob Marley labels the heavy chains which weigh him down, as the "chains of Greed." Thus, these bleak and hefty chains ultimately come to symbolise greed and avarice. Jacob Marley's chain is a long and "ponderous" one, reflecting the extent of the selfishness and opportunism he fostered in life. If Scrooge does not amend his ways, he too will descend into the afterlife bound by the same constraints. Dickens uses these chains as a **metaphoric symbol for the way in which greed permanently tarnishes individuals,** and only causes them woe in the long-term.

The Ghosts

Dickens uses the three spirits as symbols for the key moral lessons which Scrooge learns. In his first journey, Scrooge learns the way in which his past memories and experiences have shaped his present self, and how his boyhood may have sowed the seeds of his underlying bitterness. His second voyage establishes a juxtaposition between his own wealthy yet unhappy life, and the poor yet content lives of others (including his nephew Fred and the Cratchit household). Dickens suggests that wealth is not a prerequisite for happiness, but rather, that merriment is derived from non-material means. Lastly, in his third voyage, Scrooge recognises the futility of wealth in the face of isolation and abandonment, as well as the malleable nature of the future. Just like the third spirit's obscure and undefined form, so too is the future elusive in nature, and can be re-shaped by actions of the present.

The two children: Ignorance and Want

The two children which emerge from the Ghost of Christmas Present's robe are sickly, warped, deformed, and hideous, starkly juxtaposing the archetypal sweetness and gentleness of a child. These two children each symbolise want and ignorance respectively, and are described by the spirit as the product of mankind.

Dickens thus presents these two temptations as a vital threat to the integrity and empathy of mankind. The spirit warns Scrooge to beware of Ignorance most. This would imply that selfish apathy is one of man's greatest downfalls, and further perpetuates misgivings of greed and opportunism. It is ultimately Scrooge's inability to comprehend the struggle of the poor which augments his ingrained avarice.

Turkey and food

Food, and turkey specifically, symbolise wealth and prosperity in *A Christmas Carol.* Throughout the novella, there a several seemingly inconsequential references to gastronomy. Yet these references in fact serve the greater purpose of drawing a distinguishable **dichotomy** between the rich and the poor.

Dichotomy: a contrast between two things that are mutually exclusive or complete opposites.

In the scenes depicting the busy streets of London, there is an extended reference to various goods and commodities in shop windows: plums, spices, turkeys, fruits and more. Moreover, when Scrooge initially enters the room in his house to find the second spirit, he sees the Ghost of Christmas Present surrounded by a great pile of foods and sweets. These items are all inevitably accessible to the middle and upper classes only, and remain largely unreachable by the poor.

This becomes apparent above all in the third stave, where Scrooge witnesses the humble dinner at the Cratchit household on Christmas Day. Unlike the excess and abundance of food in the London shop windows, the Cratchits enjoy potatoes, a small Turkey, and an even smaller pudding. It is evident, that the meal is incredibly meagre and unfulfilling for such a large family. Yet not one member of the Cratchit household complains, and each feels sustained not only by the food itself but by the company of each other.

Likewise, Fezziwig's Christmas party is not necessarily abound with foods and goods, yet each party-goer exalts the celebration and is appreciative of Fezziwig's merry and optimistic personality.

As such, when Scrooge chooses to send the prize turkey to the Cratchit household in the fifth stave, which is twice the size of Tiny Tim, Scrooge is providing them with a commodity otherwise entirely inaccessible to the poor. Unlike the meagre meal provided to them in the spirit's vision, the family will now dine heartily.

Fire and light

Throughout literary history, fire and light has always been synonymous with positive attributes: usually happiness, hope, and truth. By contrast, darkness and dimness have always been related to negative attributes: such as death, unhappiness, and misery. In *A Christmas Carol,* there are frequent references to both light and darkness, whether they be natural (e.g. derived from the weather) or artificial (e.g. derived from a lamp).

In the first stave, Scrooge's office and home are depicted as dark and dim, for, as Scrooge believes, "darkness is cheap." The dark atmosphere of his surroundings thus reflects Scrooge's melancholy and pessimistic nature. Scrooge also subjects himself to coldness, rarely lighting his fire as a source of warmth.

By contrast, Dickens presents the reader with imagery of the light and luminescence which light the London shop windows and houses. Unlike Scrooge, the Londoners view Christmas with happiness and prosperity, and are warmed by its moral messages.

Moreover, the Ghost of Christmas Past has a beam of light which shoots from its head. This light may be seen to figuratively symbolise notions of truth and benevolence.

The weather

The weather plays an important role in *A Christmas Carol.* Pathetic fallacy is a literary device where the weather can be said to reflect the moods and emotions of the characters or the situation in the text. In simple terms, unpleasant stormy weather may reflect the sadness of a character, while bright and sunny weather may reflect the happiness of a character. This symbolic effect of weather is no less applicable to the novella.

Though the weather in *A Christmas Carol* is most frequently depicted as chilly, biting, frosty, and stormy, it ultimately juxtaposes the warmth and happiness bought by Christmas time. For individuals like Fred, the coldness and undesirability of the weather does not quash his optimism or merriment. In *A Christmas Carol,* it is important to note the several references to the weather and weather changes.

In the fifth stave, though the air is still cold, the weather is depicted as bright and sunny. The pleasant nature of the weather thus reflects Scrooge's newfound generosity, happiness, joy, gratitude, and empathy. Whereas in the beginning of the novella, Scrooge willingly subjected himself to the frostiness of the weather, reluctant to stoke a fire. However he is permeated by warmth at the end of the novella.

Allegory

An allegory can be defined as a story or narrative which can be interpreted to possess a certain hidden meaning – in the case of *A Christmas Carol*, a moral one.

A Christmas Carol can both be perceived as a **Christian allegory,** as well as a more general **allegory for the perils of greed, and the value of generosity.**

In other words, Dickens novella is not merely an innocent Christmas story, but rather, an allegory for a more important moral message.

Narrative voice

The narrative voice adopted by Charles Dickens is a unique one, which augments the dynamic nature of the storytelling in the novella. The narrator's tone varies with the emotions of the characters: it morphs smoothly from elated, to dreary, to other various emotions. It is sometimes permeated by exclamatory statements, and in other passages, is largely devoid of them.

Dickens adopts a literary feature known as free indirect speech, where the narration is written in the third person whilst still retaining some defining elements of a first-person narrator. The author is therefore able to describe the inner thoughts and emotions of the characters, whilst staying at an observational distance. In simple terms, the third-person narrator will sometimes adopt the narrative voice of one or more of the characters. This is what allows the narrative voice to vary in its tone.

Frame narrative

A frame narrative, on its most basic level, can essentially be defined as a 'story within a story'. In other words, a frame narrative refers to the telling of a tale within a pre-existing tale itself. *A Christmas Carol* can be viewed as a frame-narrative as the novella itself is a story. Yet within this broader story, the reader is greeted with Scrooge's voyage with the three spirits, which is a separate story in itself.

Indeed, prior to the appearance of Marley's Ghost on Christmas Eve, the passage commences with the words "Once upon a time" – the archetypal beginning of any tale.

Thus, the frame narrative structure of *A Christmas Carol* serves to emphasise the allegorical moral teachings Scrooge learns in his voyages with the three spirits.

Dialogue

Dialogue can be simply defined as the interactions or exchanges between two or more people. It essentially refers to a conversation held between characters. Naturally, *A Christmas Carol* is comprised of both narration and dialogue. Whereas third-person narration retells events from an observational perspective, dialogue reveals the thoughts and opinions directly from the person themselves.

Dialogue is largely depicted between Scrooge and those who he interacts with, including his nephew, Bob Cratchit, the portly gentlemen, the three spirits, and others. Dialogue also occurs between third parties in the scenes Scrooge observes with the three spirits.

Imagery

Imagery refers to visually descriptive or figurative language in which words are essentially used to bring scenes and situations to life. The effect is that a certain 'image' is evoked in the reader's mind. As such, imagery is rife in *A Christmas Carol*, and there are examples of this literary technique to be found on every single page of the novella.

Some of the most effective uses of imagery, apply to descriptions of characters and settings. For example, in the first stave, Scrooge is depicted as a "squeezing, wrenching, grasping, scraping, clutching, covetous, old sinner!" By contrast, his nephew Fred is described to have "so heated himself with rapid walking in the fog and frost [...] that his face was ruddy and handsome, his eyes sparkled, and his breath smoked again."

Metaphor

Metaphor refers to a figure of speech in which a word or term is applied to an object or subject which is not literally or technically applicable. There are several examples of metaphor in *A Christmas Carol.* For example, Dickens uses the physical coldness of the weather as a means of elucidating the bitterness and indignation of Scrooge's character. The "cold within" Scrooge's conscious, "froze his old features, nipped his pointed nose, blue and spoke out shrewdly in his grating voice." Thus, whilst this coldness within Scrooge is not literal coldness, it nevertheless suggests the sharpness and harshness of his features.

Another metaphor is Fred's belief that at Christmas time "men and women seem by one consent to open their shut-up hearts freely." Though people's hearts are not literally shut up or constrained in any way, it is used as a metaphor to highlight the generosity and benevolence which Christmas fosters in others.

Personification

Personification is the attribution of human qualities or features to something which is otherwise non-human, or inanimate. For example, if an author were to describe the wind as 'howling' or a tree as 'stooping', this would constitute personification. Personification ultimately serves to bring a certain object or thing to life, as though it were a living and breathing human organism with emotions, thoughts, and opinions.

One example of this in *A Christmas Carol* can be seen in the first stave when the narrator describes Scrooge's room and dinner as "melancholy." Obviously, a plate of food is incapable of displaying the emotions of sadness or discontent. A plate of dinner is ultimately inanimate, devoid of any human qualities. Thus, by describing Scrooge's dinner as melancholy, the narrator seeks to emphasise that each and every single aspect of Scrooge's life is pervaded by bleakness, even something as simple and quotidian as a plate of food.

Simile

Simile is a figure of speech where one thing is compared to another thing of a different kind, usually with the words 'like' or 'as'. Some common similes include 'as brave as a lion', or 'as light as a feather.' Simile has a similar purpose and effect to a metaphor.

Scrooge is described with the simile, "self-contained, and solitary as an oyster." An oyster is ultimately a shut up and enclosed mollusc, to which freedom of movement is inaccessible. Thus, like an oyster, Scrooge is acutely isolated and alone.

Denouement

Denouement refers to the final part of a narrative in which various strands of the plot are joined together, and matters and conflicts are explicated and resolved. The fifth stave serves as the denouement of *A Christmas Carol*, seeking to conclude the moral teachings of the three spirits, and to reveal Scrooge's great character development.

Section 7

Quote Bank

Christmas

Quote	Character	Stave
"He had so heated himself with rapid walking in the fog and frost, this nephew of Scrooge's, that he was all in a glow; his face was ruddy and handsome; his eyes sparkled, and his breath smoked again."	Narrator	1
"Christmas time [...] a kind, forgiving, charitable, pleasant time"	Fred	1
"Men and women by one consent to open their shut-up hearts freely"	Fred	1
"The brightness of the shops where holly sprigs and berries crackled in the lamp heat of the windows, made pale faced ruddy as they passed."	Narrator	1
"The warehouse was as snug, and warm, and dry, and bright a ball-room, as you would desire to see upon a winter's night."	Narrator	2
"A positive light appeared to issue from Fezziwig's calves. They shone in every part of the dance like moons."	Narrator	2
"During the whole of this time, Scrooge had acted like a man out of his wits. His heart and soul were in the scene, and with his former self. He corroborated everything, remembered everything, enjoyed everything, and underwent the strangest agitation."	Narrator	2
"He has spent but a few pounds of your mortal money: three or four perhaps. Is that so much that he deserves this praise?"	Ghost of Christmas Past	2
"He has the power to render us happy or unhappy; to make our service light or burdensome; a pleasure or a toil. Say that his power lies in words and looks; in things so slight and insignificant that it is impossible to add and count them up: what then? The happiness he gives, is quite as great as if it cost a fortune."	Scrooge	2

"There was nothing very cheerful in the climate or the town, and yet was there an air of cheerfulness abroad that the clearest summer air and brightest summer sun might have endeavoured to diffuse in vain."	Narrator	3
"The people who were shovelling away on the housetops were jovial and full of glee."	Narrator	3
"The scales descending on the counter made a merry sound, or that the twine and roller parted company so briskly, or that the canisters were rattled up and down like juggling tricks, or even that the blended scents of tea and coffee were so grateful to the nose."	Narrator	3
"When Scrooge's nephew laughed in this way: holding his sides, rolling his head, and twisting his face into the most extravagant contortions: Scrooge's niece, by marriage, laughed as heartily as he. And their assembled friends being not a bit behindhand, roared out lustily."	Narrator	3
"It is good to be children sometimes, and never better than at Christmas, when its mighty Founder was a child himself."	Narrator	3
"They all played, and so did Scrooge, for, wholly forgetting the interest he had in what was going on, that his voice made no sound in their ears, he sometimes came out with his guess quite loud."	Narrator	3
"Uncle Scrooge had imperceptibly become so gay and light of heart, that he would have pledged the unconscious company in return, and thanked them in an inaudible speech."	Narrator	3
"I will honour Christmas in my heart, and try to keep it all the year. I will live in the Past, the Present, and the Future. The Spirits of all Three shall strive within me. I will not shut out the lessons that they teach. Oh, tell me I may sponge away the writing on this stone!"	Narrator	5
"May that be truly said of us, and all of us! And so, as Tiny Tim observed, God bless Us, Every One!"	Narrator	5

Compassion and forgiveness

Quote	Character	Stave
"To hear Scrooge expending all the earnestness of his nature on such subjects, in a most extraordinary voice between laughing and crying; and to see his heightened and excited face; would have been a surprise to his business friends in the city, indeed."	Narrator	2
"There was a boy singing a Christmas Carol at my door last night. I should like to have given him something: that's all."	Narrator	2
"I should like to be able to say a word or two to my clerk just now! That's all."	Scrooge	2
"Ghost of the Future! [...] I fear you more than any spectre I have seen. But as I know your purpose is to do me good, and as I hope to live to be another man from what I was, I am prepared to bear you company, and do it with a thankful heart."	Scrooge	4
"'I'll send it to Bob Cratchit's!' whispered Scrooge, rubbing his hands, and splitting with a laugh. 'He sha'n't know who sends it. It's twice the size of Tiny Tim.'"	Scrooge	5
"Scrooge was better than his word. He did it all, and infinitely more; and to Tiny Tim, who did NOT die, he was a second father."	Narrator	5

Family

Quote	Character	Stave
"He told me, coming home, that he hoped the people saw him in the church, because he was a cripple, and it might be pleasant to them to remember upon Christmas Day, who made lame beggars walk, and blind men see."	Bob	2
"Bob's voice was tremulous when he told them this, and trembled more when he said that Tiny Tim was growing strong and hearty."	Narrator	2
"Its tenderness and flavour, size and cheapness, were the themes of universal admiration."	Narrator	2

"Everybody had something to say about it, but nobody said or thought it was at all a small pudding for a large family."	Narrator	2
"God bless us every one!"	Tiny Tim	2
"I know, my dears, that when we recollect how patient and how mild he was; although he was a little, little child; we shall not quarrel easily among ourselves, and forget poor Tiny Tim in doing it."	Bob	4

Greed and generosity

Quote	Character	Stave
"And even Scrooge was not dreadfully cut up by the sad event, but that he was an excellent man of business on the very day of the funeral, and solemnised it with an undoubted bargain."	Narrator	1
"Sometimes people new to the business called Scrooge Scrooge, and sometimes Marley, but he answered to both names: it was all the same to him."	Narrator	1
"A squeezing, wrenching, grasping, scraping, clutching, covetous, old sinner!'"	Narrator	1
"Hard and sharp as flint, from which no steel had ever struck out generous fire; secret, and self-contained, and solitary as an oyster."	Narrator	1
"The cold within him froze his old features, nipped his pointed nose, shrivelled his cheek, stiffened his gait; made his eyes red, his thin lips blue and spoke out shrewdly in his grating voice."	Narrator	1
"He carried his own low temperature always about him; he iced his office in the dogdays; and didn't thaw it one degree at Christmas."	Narrator	1
"To edge his way along the crowded paths of life, warning all human sympathy to keep its distance, was what the knowing ones call 'nuts' to Scrooge."	Narrator	1
"Scrooge had a very small fire, but the clerk's fire was so very much smaller that it looked like one coal."	Narrator	1

"What right have you to be dismal? What reason have you to be morose? You're rich enough."	Bob	1
"Every idiot who goes about with 'Merry Christmas' on his lips, should be boiled with his own pudding, and buried with a stake of holly through his heart."	Scrooge	1
"I don't make merry myself at Christmas and I can't afford to make idle people merry."	Scrooge	1
"'If they would rather die,' said Scrooge, 'they had better do it, and decrease the surplus population.'"	Scrooge	1
"Darkness is cheap, and Scrooge liked it."	Narrator	1
"It is a ponderous chain!"	Marley	1
"'But you were always a good man of business, Jacob,' faltered Scrooge, who now began to apply this to himself."	Scrooge	1
"There was an eager, greedy, restless motion in the eye, which showed the passion that had taken root, and where the shadow of the growing tree would fall."	Narrator	2
"There is nothing on which it is so hard as poverty; and there is nothing it professes to condemn with such severity as the pursuit of wealth!"	Scrooge	2
"I have seen your nobler aspirations fall off one by one, until the master-passion, Gain, engrosses you."	Belle	2
"You were another man."	Belle	2
"In an changed nature; in an altered spirit; in another atmosphere of life; another Hope as its great end."	Belle	2
"A tremendous family to provide for."	Scrooge	3
"If these shadows remain unaltered by the Future, none other of my race [...] will find him here. What then? If he be like to die, he had better do it, and decrease the surplus population."	Ghost of Christmas Present	3
"Scrooge hung his head to hear his own words quoted by the Spirit, and was overcome with penitence and grief."	Narrator	3

Isolation

Quote	Character	Stave
"Scrooge took his melancholy dinner in his usual melancholy tavern; and having read all the newspapers [...] went home to bed."	Narrator	1
"Your lip is trembling [...] and what is that upon your cheek?"	Ghost of Christmas Past	2
"What was merry Christmas to Scrooge? Out upon merry Christmas! What good had it ever done to him?"	Narrator	2
"A solitary child, neglected by his friends, is left there still."	Ghost of Christmas Past	2
"It opened before them, and disclosed a long, bare, melancholy room, made barer still by lines of plain deal forms and desks. At one of these a lonely was reading near a feeble fire; and Scrooge sat down upon a form, and wept to see his poor forgotten self as he used to be."	Narrator	2
"Father is so much kinder than he used to be, that home's like Heaven!"	Fran	2
"I could scarcely help seeing him. His partner lies upon the point of death, I hear; and there he sat alone. Quite alone in the world, I do believe."	Belle's husband	2
"However, his offences carry their own punishment, and I have nothing to say against him."	Fred	3
"'What of that, my dear?' said Scrooge's nephew. 'His wealth is of no use to him. He don't do any good with it. He don't make himself comfortable with it.'"	Fred	3
"The consequence of his taking a dislike to us, and not making merry with us, is, as I think, that he loses some pleasant moments, which could do him no harm. I am sure he loses pleasanter companions than he can find in his own thoughts, either in his mouldy old office, or his dusty chambers."	Fred	3
"'It's likely to be a very cheap funeral,' said the same speaker; 'for upon my life I don't know of anybody to go to it. Suppose we make up a party and volunteer?'"	Business-man	4

"If he wanted to keep them after he was dead, a wicked old screw [...] why wasn't he natural in his lifetime? If he had been, he'd have had somebody to look after him when he was struck with Death, instead of lying gasping out his last there, alone by himself."	Pawnshop woman	4
"She was a mild and patient creature if her face spoke truth; but she was thankful in her soul to hear it, and she said so, with clasped hands. She prayed forgiveness the next moment, and was sorry; but the first was the emotion of her heart."	Narrator	4

Social inequity: Victorian society

Quote	Character	Stave
"Many thousands are in want of common necessaries; hundreds of thousands are in want of common comforts, sir."	Portly gentleman	1
"Sending out a meagre servant to offer a glass of 'something' to the postboy, who answered that he thanked the gentleman, but if it was the same tap he had tasted before, he had rather not."	Narrator	2
"I wonder you, of all the beings in the many worlds about us, should desire to cramp these people's opportunities of innocent enjoyment."	Scrooge	3
"'There are some upon this earth of yours,' returned the Spirit, 'who lay claim to know us, and who do their deeds of passion, pride, ill-will, hatred, envy, bigotry, and selfishness in our name, who are as strange to us and all our kith and kin, as if they had never lived. Remember that, and charge their doings on themselves, not us.'"	Ghost of Christmas Present	3
"Then up rose Mrs Cratchit, Cratchit's wife, dressed out but poorly in a twice-turned gown, but brave in ribbons, which are cheap and make a goodly show for sixpence."	Narrator	3
"It should be Christmas Day, I am sure [...] on which one drinks the health of such an odious, stingy, hard, unfeeling man as Mr Scrooge. You know he is, Robert. Nobody knows it better than you do, poor fellow."	Mrs Cratchit	3

"There was nothing of high mark in this. They were not a handsome family; they were not well dressed; their shoes were far from being water-proof; their clothes were scanty; and Peter might have known, and very likely did, the inside of a pawnbroker's. But, they were happy, grateful, pleased with one another, and contented with the time."	Narrator	3
"They were a boy and a girl. Yellow, meagre, ragged, scowling, wolfish; but prostrate, too, in their humility."	Narrator	3
"They are Man's [...] and they cling to me, appealing from their fathers. This boy is Ignorance. This girl is Want. Beware them both, and all of their degree, but most of all beware this boy, for on his brow I see that written which is Doom, unless the writing be erased."'	Ghost of Christmas Present	3
"They were men of aye business: very wealthy, and of great importance. He had made a point always of standing well in their esteem: in a business point of view, that is; strictly in a business point of view."	Narrator	4
"The ways were foul and narrow; the shops and houses wretched; the people half-naked, drunken, slipshod, ugly. Alleys and archways, like so many cesspools, disgorged their offenses of smell, and dirt, and life, upon the straggling streets; and the whole quarter reeked with crime, with filth, and misery."	Narrator	4

Time: past, present, and future

Quote	Character	Stave
"Old Marley was as dead as a door-nail."	Narrator	1
"There is no doubt that Marley was dead. This must be distinctly understood, or nothing wonderful can come of the story I am going to relate."	Narrator	1
"Marley's face. It was not in impenetrable shadow as the other objects in the yard were, but had a dismal light about it, like a bad lobster in a dark cellar."	Narrator	1
"A clanking noise, deep down below; as if some person were dragging a heavy chain over the casks."	Narrator	1

"If that spirit goes not forth in life, it is condemned to do so after death. It is doomed to wander through the world."	Narrator	1
"Without their visits [...] you cannot hope to shun the path I tread."	Marley	1
"The air was filled with phantoms, wandering hither and thither in restless haste, and moaning as they went. Every one of them wore chains like Marley's Ghost."	Narrator	1
"It was a strange figure – like a child: yet not so like a child as like an old man, viewed through some supernatural medium, which gave him the appearance of having receded from the view, and being diminished to a child's proportions. Its hair, which hung about its neck and down its back, was white as if with age; and yet the face had not a wrinkle in it, and the tenderest bloom was on the skin."	Narrator	2
"From the crown of its head there sprung a bright clear jet of light, by which all was visible, and which was doubtless the occasion of its using, in its duller moments, a great extinguisher for a cap"	Narrator	2
"He was conscious of a thousand odours floating in the air, each one connected with a thousand thoughts, and hopes, and joys, and cares long, long, forgotten."	Narrator	2
"Scrooge pressed it down with all his force, he could not hide the light, which streamed from under it, in an unbroken flood upon the ground."	Narrator	2
"There sat a jolly Giant, glorious to see: who bore a glowing torch, in shape not unlike Plenty's horn, and held it up, high up, to shed light on Scrooge."	Narrator	3
"I see a vacant seat [...] in the poor chimney-corner, and a crutch without an owner, carefully preserved. If these shadows remain unaltered by the Future, the child will die."	Ghost of Christmas Present	3
"Scrooge crept towards it, trembling as he went; and following the finger, read upon the stone of the neglected grave his own name, EBENEZER SCROOGE."	Narrator	4

Section 8

Sample Essays

Essay One

QUESTION: "A solitary child, neglected by his friends, is left there still.'"
In *A Christmas Carol,* Scrooge's bitter character cannot be attributed to greed alone. Discuss.

ESSAY	COMMENTS
INTRODUCTION Charles Dickens' seminal novella *A Christmas Carol* depicts the character of Ebenezer Scrooge at the forefront of the frame narrative.[1] Portrayed as an opportunistic and avarice-driven old man, Scrooge's bitterness may seem, on the surface, to derive solely from greed.[2] However, Scrooge's isolating childhood, as well as his ignorance, also play a role in his indignant attitude. Dickens' novella is set in the Victorian era at Christmas time, whereby a dichotomy between the rich and the poor is established, alluding to the great class chasm of the era.[3] Dickens thus cautions against the perils of greed, yet he also posits that for characters like Scrooge, this avarice stems from more deep-rooted issues.[4]	1. Mentioning the frame narrative in the novella engages with the notion of form. It is important to demonstrate your structural knowledge of the text. It is often easiest to do so in the introduction, where we lay out 'foundational' concepts. 2. This sentence directly engages with the prompt. We are developing our stance on the topic. In this instance, we are agreeing with the prompt, yet somewhat negating it by also emphasising that Scrooge's greed plays a crucial role in his bitterness. 3. Here, we have established context. Whilst it is usually preferable to introduce context in the second or third sentence, sometimes, introducing later is warranted. 4. This sentence engages with 'big picture' ideas and authorial intent by considering what message Dickens wanted to convey to readers.

PARAGRAPH 1	
Though Scrooge's harsh nature cannot be solely attributed to greed, this avarice nevertheless plays a significant role in his acerbic conduct.[5] Scrooge is not only intrinsically frugal with others, but also with himself.[6] By denying even himself any indulgence in his great wealth, he perpetuates a deep-seated discontent. Whilst the second, third, fourth and fifth staves serve to reveal Scrooge's miraculous character development, the first stave elucidates the confronting extent of his greed. Scrooge chooses to fester in a literal and metaphorical dimness,[7] refusing to provide his household or office with ample light, under the justification that "darkness is cheap." Even his fire in his counting-house is "very small" – though his clerk Bob Cratchit's is "very much smaller." As such, Scrooge is not only "hard and sharp as flint" with others, but also with himself. Of course however, this desire to covetously hoard his own wealth extends to his conduct with others. The narrator reveals that Scrooge was "not so dreadfully cut up by the sad event" of the death of his long-term business partner Jacob Marley, but rather, mulled on the fact that "he was an excellent man of business." The funeral is not an expensive one, despite his overwhelming wealth, but rather, is performed for an "undoubted bargain." Moreover, his greed causes him to selfishly deny any monetary compensation for those less fortunate than he. Despite the evident poorness and economic struggle of his clerk, Scrooge staunchly refuses to raise his pay. Instead, he condemns Christmas as a "poor excuse for picking a man's pocket" – though it only occurs once a year.	5. Our topic sentence makes it clear that we are *challenging* the prompt, but not *dodging* the question. Even though we're arguing that greed isn't the only motivating factor, we're still focusing much of our discussion on greed (rather than veering off course to discuss other themes, which some teachers might penalise you for!). Always remember to stick to the scope of the essay question and build out your discussion from there! 6. Here, we're expanding on the idea of greed by pointing out that Scrooge doesn't just deprive others of things – he also deprives himself, which allows for a more in-depth discussion of his character's psychology. 7. Remember than in this text, light and dark are often deeply symbolic.

Thus, Scrooge, a "squeezing, wrenching, grasping, scraping, clutching, covetous old sinner," derives much of his bitterness from the ingrained desire to harvest his money at all costs. Yet, his more than deficient generosity to the poor, including Bob Cratchit, can also be attributed to his ignorance.[8] **PARAGRAPH 2** Ignorance also plays a significant role in Scrooge's bitter character. In the third stave, the Ghost of Christmas Present warns against the perils of the two children which squander at his feet in misery: Want and Ignorance. Though he cautions against Want (or greed), he cautions even more so against Ignorance, suggesting it is one of the most fatal flaws prone to man. Scrooge, ignorant to the extent of the struggles of the poor and less fortunate, treats such individuals with impatient neglect, choosing to view his surroundings through his own narrow lens of wealth. As such, when Scrooge witnesses the scenes of those less fortunate than he in his voyage with the second spirit, his bitterness further collapses into empathetic understanding, Scrooge asks the Spirit why he "of all beings in the many worlds about us" would openly choose to "cramp these people's opportunities of innocent enjoyment."[9]	8. This is a strong linking sentence, which links both backwards and forwards. In other words, it further clarifies what has already been discussed in the paragraph, whilst simultaneously touching on the argument which is yet to be explored in the second body paragraph. Linking sentences help in establishing an overall continuity in your essay, ensuring that the transition from paragraph to paragraph is not jarring or awkward in any way. 9. Notice that most of these quotes are less than ten words each, with paraphrasing to help keep quotes as concise as possible? This ensures the marker can see we're being precise with our use of evidence.

The spirit incredulously counters that it is the lack of sympathetic understanding of humans, which in reality contributes to their suffering. Scrooge, therefore, had failed to see his moral responsibility when he denied the portly gentlemen their donations, and Bob Cratchit his raised salary, in the first stave. As such, when he witnesses the humble nature of the Cratchit's Christmas dinner – comprising a small turkey, some meagre potatoes and an even smaller pudding – he recognises the undeserved suffering of the working classes. Dickens therefore, elucidates the way in which ignorance can blunt sympathy and empathy, and perpetuate bitterness.[10] **PARAGRAPH 3** Besides greed and ignorance, Scrooge's isolation cannot be ignored in the formation of his bitter character. Scrooge's journey with the Ghost of Christmas Past in the second stave reveals the way in which this solitude stemmed from his boyhood. The imagery of the "long, bare, melancholy room" in which Scrooge sat alone at his school emphasises the isolating quality of his childhood.[11] Scrooge's small, childlike figure is juxtaposed by the great empty expanse of the room. The narrator describes Scrooge as a "lonely boy reading near a feeble fire," in stark contrast to the previous imagery of the schoolboys "in great spirits" who "shouted to each other" in glee. Moreover, the subsequent scene with his younger sister Fran's arrival alludes to the austere nature of his father. Fran exclaims that "father is so much minder than he used to be," pointing towards his bitter and indignant nature. Ironically, this can be closely compared to Scrooge's own indignance in his household.	10. This is an authorial statement. An authorial statement refers to any sentence or phrase which describes what the author is doing in writing the text (e.g. 'Dickens highlights/ suggests/ illustrates...' etc.). Authorial statements lend themselves towards discussing the overall message of the text, and are the perfect way to wrap up your body paragraphs. 11. Here, we have referred to imagery (a literary technique). Though quotes will always be your 'typical' form of evidence, it is also important that you occasionally turn to literary techniques as well to demonstrate your grasp of the overall text, not just some of the dialogue.

Thus, although Scrooge cannot be entirely absolved of his sinful harshness, it is evident that it has its origins in his early experiences.[12] Moreover, though Scrooge undergoes an "alteration" of character in his early adulthood, justifying his fiancée Belle's decision to leave him, he his nevertheless abandoned once more. Perhaps then , Scrooge's previous experiences of isolation inform his willing solitude in his adulthood, perpetuated a bitter character which festers in prolonged discontent and remorse. **CONCLUSION** Ultimately, Scrooge's bitterness cannot be derived from one driving factor alone. Whilst greed and avarice certainly augment his harsh and biting ways, his deep-seated ignorance and long-standing isolation also inform his spiteful manner. As such, Dickens warns against these three factors as perilous perpetuators of human indignance.[13]	12. This further shows that we have expanded our discussion from the prompt's starting point, as we've gone beyond simply examining how Scrooge *is* greedy and have delved into *why* he is greedy. 13. This conclusion is short and sweet, but approximately three sentences is all you need! Short conclusions are often most effective, as they allow you to communicate and summarise your ideas swiftly, without repeating yourself. The last sentence also refers to a 'big picture' idea, extending the scope of the prompt beyond the narrow confines that it poses.

Essay Two

QUESTION: "If they would rather die," said Scrooge, "they had better do it, and decrease the surplus population."
To what extent does Charles Dickens critique the ignorance of Victorian society in *A Christmas Carol?*

ESSAY	COMMENTS
INTRODUCTION Charles Dickens' novella *A Christmas Carol* is a cautionary tale against the woeful perils of selfish ignorance. Dickens ultimately condemns selfish incomprehension[1] as a perpetuator of greed and indignance, exemplified through the bitter character of Scrooge. *A Christmas Carol* is anchored in the Victorian era, where there was a stark divide between the rich and the poor, in which the middle and upper classes would exploit the manpower and desperation of the working classes.[2] Thus, Dickens' novella serves as a societal critique, imploring the subjects of ignorance to open their eyes to need for sympathy and benevolence.	1. It's good to introduce synonyms or related key terms for major themes like 'ignorance' that appear in the prompt. This helps you showcase your understanding of what these themes mean, while also ensuring your writing doesn't get too repetitive. 2. This sentence contextualises the novella, whilst simultaneously adhering to the prompt. Given that the prompt requires you to explore the notion of 'Victorian society', it is necessary to tap into this idea by explaining various aspects of this era.

PARAGRAPH 1	
Dickens denounces the way in which ignorance blunts the empathy of individuals with respect to the poor and less fortunate. Scrooge, above all, is the ultimate embodiment of this sympathetic deficiency. When the portly gentlemen confront Scrooge for donations to the "Poor and destitute" of London, Scrooge engages in a sardonic dialogue, insensitively suggesting that the London poor seek the aid of the "prisons" and "Union workhouses." Scrooge then quashes the efforts of the gentlemen altogether, cruelly arguing that if "they would rather die" than reside in these public institutions, then "they had better do it, and decrease the surplus population."[3] Unwilling to witness, or at least conceptualise, the suffering of the less fortunate, Scrooge's ignorance causes him to harvest and covet his wealth. Ironically, when this ignorance is unveiled in his voyage with the Ghost of Christmas Present, Scrooge his ashamed to have his own words spoken to him once more. After witnessing the "poor revellers" of London with their humble dinners, Scrooge recognises the unjust class divide which pervades Victorian society. Scrooge questions why "these people's opportunities of innocent enjoyment" should be "cramp[ed]." Likewise, when Scrooge desperately enquires whether "Tiny Tim will live," the Ghost curtly echoes Scrooge's own previous sentiments: "if he be like to die, he had better do it, and decrease the surplus population." It is only when Scrooge's ignorance (symbolic for broader Victorian ignorance), is dissolved with living experience, that he becomes capable of sympathy and empathy.[4]	3. Here, we are directly engaging with the quote in the prompt. It is important not to completely neglect the attached quote, as technically, it is part of the question itself. If it is not addressed in the introduction, it should certainly be addressed in one of the body paragraphs. You can think of the quote as a kind of hint that answers the question: in this case, to what extent is Dickens criticising ignorance? Well, here's a quote in which Scrooge is being so ignorant and callous that he's later embarrassed to hear the words thrown back at him, so clearly Dickens is presenting us with a scathing critique of such attitudes! 4. It is important to always link back to the topic. In this specific prompt, we have the bifold task of addressing both the notion of 'ignorance' and 'Victorian society,' and both are equally important. Try to address how these concepts relate to one another too – don't just write about each idea in a separate paragraph, as this makes it harder to tie everything together and explore your overarching interpretation or thesis.

PARAGRAPH 2	
By constructing a stark dichotomy between the rich and the poor in *A Christmas Carol*, Dickens highlights the apathetic[5] attitude of London's wealthy. Whilst the poor continue to squander in poverty, the rich pass idly by with no sense of moral obligation. Throughout his novella, Dickens constantly employs language which distinguishes the poor from the rich, whether explicitly or implicitly. Food, for example, becomes symbolic of an individual's social status.[6] Whilst the Cratchits dine on a small turkey and an even smaller pudding, scarcely large enough to satisfy a "large family," the London shop windows are filled with "tea and coffee," "raisins," "almonds," "sticks of cinnamon," "candied fruits," and "French plums."[7] Thus, while the wealthy may gorge on all manner of Christmas delicacies, the poor are confined to a meagre fraction of these commodities. Nevertheless however, humble families like the Cratchits are not trumped in their ability to enjoy the spirit of Christmas. On the contrary, they are consumed not by greed but by gratitude, with the most unfortunate of all, Tiny Tim, passionately exclaiming "God bless us, every one!" In the fifth stave, the "prize turkey" which Scrooge sends to the Cratchit household is no economic sacrifice for Scrooge, yet is certainly a reverent blessing for the Cratchits. Through this, Dickens therefore critiques the ignorant selfishness of the Victorian rich, and examines the bitter truth that the wealthy cannot truly appreciate what they have in the same way the poor can.[8]	5. This is a great word to use when discussing societal attitudes, and creates a good link between the previous paragraph's discussion of sympathy and empathy. 6. It is important not to loose sight of literary techniques. Symbolism is often useful, as it more easily allows you to connect form and content. 7. Employing quotes in a list like this is often incredibly useful and efficient. It allows you to display a breadth of information, without making your writing extremely clunky and jarring. 8. Linking back to the topic is often as simple as inserting some brief words/vocab. Here, speaking specifically about 'the Victorian rich' means we're making a clear reference to the essay question, contextualising the discussion and securing more marks!

PARAGRAPH 3	
Moreover,[9] Dickens condemns the way in which ignorance blinds individuals to the futility of wealth and opportunism. Scrooge, sheltered in his own insular and covetous world, fails to consider the non-material assets which lie beyond money. In his journey with the Ghost of Christmas Past, Scrooge recognises the significance of human benevolence and joviality, over wealth and frugality. The Christmas Party which Scrooge's old boss Fezziwig hosts is scarcely an indulgent or excessive one, with only but "a few pounds" of expense. The spirit probingly questions Scrooge as to why "these silly folks [are] so full of gratitude" over a "small matter." Scrooge, now recognising the relative insignificance of "mortal money" in comparison to Fezziwig's spirit, champions the way in which Fezziwig "has the power to render us happy or unhappy, to make our service light or burdensome, a pleasure or a toil." Ironically, it is Scrooge's avarice-driven attitude, contrary to Fezziwig's, which causes his previous fiancé Belle to leave him. Ignorant to the futility of wealth, young Scrooge now has an "eager, greedy, restless motion in the eye." Dickens therefore critiques the way in which the "nobler aspirations" of Victorian society have given way to the ignorant "master passion, Gain."	9. Though this may seem too good to be true, a single linking word like 'Moreover' or 'Furthermore' at the start of a new body paragraph can make your overall essay flow much better for your marker. Obviously it's still important that your ideas and sentences flow together too, but don't neglect these simple linking words in facilitating a nice, smooth reading experience!

Moreover, Scrooge's journey with the Ghost of Christmas Yet to Come unveils the solicitude and isolation produced from futile wealth. Scrooge is ultimately shunned in death for his bitterness in life, and his wealth serves him no useful purpose. Indeed, a lifetime of money-making earns him a painful and lonely death, devoid of "somebody to look after him when he was struck in Death, instead of lying gasping out his last there, alone by himself." As such, Dickens disparages[10] blind ignorance to the futile nature of avarice.

CONCLUSION

Whilst Dickens *A Christmas Carol* may depict a fictional London, he nevertheless employs his novella as an allegory[11] for the perils of greed which afflict Victorian society. Whilst characters like Scrooge and Jacob Marley represent the Victorian rich, individuals like the Cratchits embody the pitiful London poor. Ignorance towards the struggles of the "Poor and destitute" is ultimately conveyed as a perilous deed which yields unwelcomed consequences for the antagonists. Through Scrooge's own moral awakening by the visits of the three ghosts, Dickens also encourages a moral awakening for Victorian society at large.[12]

10. Remember to have synonyms on hand for frequently used words (particularly for those in the prompt). Here, we have used the verb 'disparages' to replace the word 'critiques.' Other synonyms may include condemns, castigates, admonishes, denounces, etc.

11. Here, we have a reference to form. It is important not to neglect the overall characteristics and purposes of the novella. Specifying that the novella is an allegory not only achieves this broader concept, but also links in smoothly to the prompt.

12. By establishing this parallel between a central character and the reader (our specific reader in this case includes Victorians), we are addressing the requirements of the prompt.

Essay Three

QUESTION: "And so, as Tiny Tim observed, God bless us, every one!" How does Charles Dickens convey the significance of Christmas spirit in *A Christmas Carol?*

ESSAY	COMMENTS
INTRODUCTION In *A Christmas Carol*, Charles Dickens foregrounds the true definition of the idealised Christmas spirit comes to the forefront of the novella. Dickens employs the inherent selfishness of Scrooge as a broader critique of the middle-upper classes of 19th century London, serving to contrast the optimism and festive joy of fundamental characters like Tiny Tim, Fezziwig, Belle, Fran, and Fred. It is through these characters, the visits of the three spirits and Scrooge's dramatic character arc, that Dickens defines and illuminates the vital significance of Christmas spirit. For Dickens, Christmas spirit extends beyond the brief festive season itself, and provides a model for year-long generosity, compassion and gratitude.[1]	1. It is important to describe what a 'Christmas spirit' actually is within the context of the novella. Without explaining the specific meaning behind this broad term, you will be unable to truly answer the essay question. This final sentence of the introduction is brief and concise, yet simultaneously does a good job of summarising the focal point of the prompt.

PARAGRAPH 1 Dickens establishes a stark contrast between Ebenezer Scrooge's past, present and future self in an attempt to portray the decrescendo and subsequent crescendo of Scrooge's belief in Christmas and all of its associated qualities. In the first stave, Scrooge is characterised as harsh, selfish and disinterested. In essence, he is the antithesis of Christmas cheer and delight. The exclamatory litany of Scrooge as a "squeezing, wrenching, grasping, scraping, clutching, covetous, old sinner!" conjures the imagery of an angered and grouchy old man, cynical towards his surroundings.[2] Likewise, Scrooge's repetitive exclamation "humbug!" neatly summarises his dismissive attitude towards the significance of Christmas beyond gluttony, decorations and other commercial aspects. Dickens repeatedly characterises Scrooge with an air of frostiness, employing both internal and external cold as a means of figuratively reflecting his icy attitude. The imagery of the "frosty rime [...] on his forehead' and his "iced" office establish a sense of literal and metaphorical coldness. This can be juxtaposed with the typically warm and bright associations of the Christmas spirit. It is Scrooge's transformation by the fifth stave, which serves to reflect these latter ideas of warmth. He sends the "prize turkey" to the Cratchit household, makes a charitable donation to the "portly gentlemen," and arrives at Fred's house for Christmas dinner. It is not commodities and commercialism which epitomizes the meaning of Christmas spirit.[3] Rather, through Scrooge's character development, Dickens suggests that the Christmas spirit can be considered as an attitude defined by hope and compassion.	2. Here, we are engaging with the 'how' part of the prompt. A 'how' question invites you to consider the conscious choices an author has made in an attempt to establish meaning – in this case, the Christmas spirit. As such, most 'how' prompts lend themselves towards discussing literary techniques. The first body paragraph explores a couple of these, ensuring that Dickens' construction of the novella is being adequately considered. 3. Once more, we are exploring the definition of the 'Christmas spirit.' Christmas is generally associated with highly commercialised ideas of food, presents, decorations etc. Dickens however, attempts to balance these aspects with the idealised attitude of gratitude and generosity which epitomise the Christmas spirit.

PARAGRAPH 2	
The respective visits of the three Spirits each provide Scrooge with a fundamental message which form Dickens' ideal interpretation of the Christmas spirit. The Ghost of Christmas Past reveals several memories of Scrooge's childhood and young adulthood, many of which depict the typically merry and gleeful associations of Christmas. Most notably, Fezziwig's Christmas Eve party embodies the true culmination of the Christmas spirit. Though Fezziwig has spent "but a few pounds" in funding the party, it is not the commodities which contribute to the magical atmosphere. Rather, it is Fezziwig's enthusiasm and optimism which creates a "happiness [...] quite as great as if it cost a fortune." Furthermore,[4] the Ghost of Christmas Present counsels against the perils of Want and Ignorance, suggesting that the Christmas spirit must be devoid of these two human temptations. The frightening imagery of the two decrepit children which moan and drawl at the foot of the Spirit's robe, return the reader's attention back to the first stave, where Scrooge's greed and ignorance were demonstrated at best. His refusal to donate even a penny to the "Poor and destitute" of London, his cruel treatment of Bob Cratchit, and his refusal to dine at his nephew Fred's house on Christmas form the antithesis[5] of the Christmas spirit. Similarly, the Ghost of Christmas Yet to Come illuminates the futility of wealth and greed. The two sinister temptations of Want and Ignorance ultimately disintegrate into meaninglessness in death, and leave behind only a sorrowful and cruel legacy of their beholder. Dickens thus posits that the essence of the true Christmas spirit is to parade their virtues and goodwill in life, so that they may enjoy a peaceful parting.[6]	4. Note the use of linking words to smoothly transition between ideas and examples. 5. This is a great work to describe just how opposed Scrooge is to the notion of Christmas and generosity at the start of the novella. 6. Note the use of authorial sentences in this essay. In order to truly answer a 'how' question, you must constantly engage with the author's particular construction of the text. Beginning your sentences with the author's name allows you to do so in an effortless way.

Ultimately, Scrooge's voyages with the three Spirits each contribute a certain meaning to the Christmas spirit, whilst also revealing a host of characters who embody this spirit at its best.[7]

PARAGRAPH 3

Charles Dickens employs several characters as vessels of the idealistic Christmas spirit, in order to underscore its significance in contrast to the superficial commodities of Christmas, and the pessimism of characters like Scrooge. Tiny Tim, the Cratchit household, Fezziwig, Fran, Belle, and Fred are all examples of this.[8] The Cratchit family embody the virtue of gratitude and hope. Despite their economic scarcity and Tiny Tim's debilitating illness, the family enjoy their Christmas with thanksgiving and glee. Despite the meagre size of the goose and the even smaller pudding, the children are nevertheless delighted by the humble meal presented to them. In particular, Tiny Tim, despite his weak and fragile frame appears to be the most grateful of all, genuinely declaring "god bless us, every one!"[9] The fact that Dickens chooses to conclude the novella with this very exclamation, points to Tiny Tim as the greatest embodiment of true Christmas spirit. Likewise, Fezziwig embodies the necessary enthusiasm and joviality of Christmas spirit, much like Scrooge's younger sister Fran. Fred's forgiveness and optimism are also espoused by Dickens, who greets his uncle with persistent kindness despite Scrooge's bitter reluctance.

7. Just as you can link from idea to idea (as seen above), you can also link from paragraph to paragraph. This distinguishes a good linking sentence, from an average one. When you can connect your ideas between the paragraphs, you are on your way to establishing a fluid and coherent essay where everything flows seamlessly. This can be contrasted to an essay which may have some great individual ideas, but is overall jumpy and disjointed. In order to link both 'backwards' (from the current paragraph) and 'forwards' (to the next paragraph), you need to address the central ideas of both paragraphs by linking these to the prompt.

8. This is an effective listing method which condenses lots of evidence that we will then unpack in this paragraph.

9. Here, we have referred to the quote in the essay prompt in a smooth and subtle way. The accompanying quote should always be addressed somewhere in the essay, and it fits in nicely into this section where we have chosen to discuss Tiny Tim.

Rather than castigating the "old man," Fred and his family innocently tease him as reminiscent of a "bear," and wish him a sincere "Merry Christmas and an Happy New Year." As for Scrooge's former fiancé Belle, she symbolises the qualities of humility and gratitude. She condemns Scrooge's newfound greed and "changed nature," suggesting that the Christmas spirit entails more than just glee and merriment, but also encompasses deeper virtues of thanksgiving. Through these characters, Dickens seeks to establish the vital importance of Christmas spirit in a world where superficialities and commodities appear to dominate.[10]

CONCLUSION

In essence, the true meaning of Christmas spirit comes to the forefront of the novella, providing a model for the antidote to increasing selfishness and ignorance in 19th century London.[11] For Dickens, therefore, Christmas spirit is more than an attitude which should be adopted strictly during the festive season. Rather, it is a permanent and lasting virtue which should be carried and executed year-long.

10. It is important to always tie the conclusion of the paragraph back to the prompt. It is not enough to simply discuss 'Christmas spirit' generally. Rather, we must discuss its *'significance.'*

11. Whilst referring back to the context may be somewhat irrelevant for certain essay prompts, it is quite significant here. We must consider Dickens's novella as a quasi critique of the middle-upper classes of 19th century London, rather than an entirely separate tale with no links to his contemporary society.

Essay Four

QUESTION: "Scrooge was better than his word. He did it all, and infinitely more." How is the character of Scrooge influenced by the three spirits in *A Christmas Carol?*

ESSAY	COMMENTS
INTRODUCTION In Charles Dickens' novella *A Christmas Carol,* Ebenezer Scrooge has his sense of self and world view reformed by the visits of three spirits. Each of the three voyages plays an integral role in eroding his cruel and bitter nature, and augmenting his sense of compassion and gratitude. It is perhaps through these Spirits, that Dickens seeks to critique the middle-upper class of 19th century London, increasingly submerged in an environment of capitalism. Through learning the futility of greed, the perils of ignorance, and the true meaning of the Christmas spirit, Scrooge becomes an entirely changed man from the three elusive ghosts.[1] **PARAGRAPH 1** The meaninglessness of excessive greed and wealth is above all revealed by the Ghost of Christmas Yet to Come, who takes Scrooge on a grim and dull journey into future events. Scrooge is exposed to several scenes, whereby not one individual is saddened or grieved by his hypothetical death.	1. This sentence has efficiently and concisely set out the three arguments of the essay. Some students will simply have one paragraph dedicated to each of the spirits, and although this isn't necessarily wrong, it is a fairly simple approach that may suggest a lack of confidence in developing three cogent and unique arguments, so try to ensure your paragraphs always concentrate on ideas, not just characters.

Indeed, the "only emotion that the ghost could show him" related to Scrooge's death, "was one of pleasure." The indifference of Scrooge's former businessmen, the eagerness of the thieves in the pawnshop, and the relief of the indebted husband and wife all point towards[2] the futility of Scrooge's obsession with wealth and affluence. His bountiful earnings and possessions are all ultimately rendered useless in his death – condemned by the Ghost of Christmas Past as "mortal money." This can be contrasted[3] to the death of Tiny Tim, whose grim departure establishes "a tenderness connected with a death," unlike that of Scrooge's. Though the Cratchit household is poor and penniless, they vouch to not "forget Tiny Tim." Dickens thus suggest that family and Christmas values, are ultimately superior to any cursory pleasure bought by wealth. As such, he warns against the perils of "Want," embodied by the hideous and disfigured child clinging to the robe of the Ghost of Christmas Present.[4] **PARAGRAPH 2** Furthermore, in the third stave, the Ghost of Christmas Present reveals not just the child of "Want," but also one of "Ignorance."[5] Scrooge therefore also learns of the perils of this latter sinful temptation. Scrooge's cruel indifference towards the hardships of others is made clear in the first stave. Most notably, he denies a donation to the portly gentleman for the "Poor and destitute" of London, cruelly suggesting that they seek refuge in the "prisons" and "union workhouses."	2. Collecting similar evidence together in a sentence like this makes for a very efficient means of covering the whole text. 3. Finding points of difference can be just as useful in creating links within a body paragraph as points of similarity. 4. Though this paragraph has largely focused on the Ghost of Christmas Yet to Come, there are also brief references to the significance of the other two spirits. Rather than confining the discussion to just one spirit, which would pose several limitations to the breadth of ideas, the discussion has been expanded. 5. This topic sentence links both backwards and forwards. That is, it establishes a connection to the final sentence of the previous paragraph, whilst simultaneously outlining the focus of the current paragraph. Sentences like this allow the essay to flow smoothly and establish coherent ideas.

It is clear, that Scrooge is entirely ignorant to the struggles faced by the less fortunate, failing to believe that some would "rather die" than flock to these public establishments.[6] However, upon witnessing Christmas dinner at the Cratchit household, Scrooge is exposed to the limitations imposed on the poor. Despite Tiny Tim's fragile and sickly frame, the family nevertheless remain in good spirits. Likewise, despite the meagre size of the turkey and pudding, they are nevertheless satisfied and grateful for the meal presented to them. Scrooge's reformation from witnessing this vision, comes to fruition in the final stave, where he makes a charitable donation to the portly gentleman, and anonymously sends over the "prize turkey" to the Cratchit household. The delight these simple actions bring Scrooge ultimately points towards the futility of ignorance and the fruitfulness of generosity. **PARAGRAPH 3** Though *A Christmas Carol* is an allegory for the selfish temptations of society in general, it also of course underscores the significance of the Christmas season itself. Through the visits of the three Spirits, Scrooge learns of the importance of the Christmas spirit, and the increased need for kindness, compassion and generosity during the festive season. This particular attitude fostered at Christmas time, is above all exemplified through the characters of Fred, Fran, Fezziwig, Belle, and Tiny Tim.	6. Remember that you can use very short quotes (especially if you find these easier to memorise). In fact, having very long quotes tends to come across as imprecise and unnecessary, so try to only isolate the most important language in the text to comment on.

Despite Scrooge's ill treatment of him, Fred is nevertheless merry with his uncle, insisting that he "dine with [them] tomorrow" on Christmas Day. Moreover, Scrooge's younger sister Fran greets him with elated excitement at his boarding school, bearing a "brimful of glee" and a "large heart." Fezziwig is capable of livening the entire room at his Christmas Eve party merely with his richness in spirit, rather than any significant commodities. Furthermore, Belle exemplifies the importance of family at Christmas time, bearing a "laughing face" in the presence of her husband and children. Perhaps most significantly, Tiny Tim's optimism elucidates the importance of gratitude to the Christmas Spirit. Though he is the weakest and smallest of all of his family members, he "heart[ily]" declares "God bless us, every one!" turning his back to any pessimism or bitterness. As such, through the visits of the three ghosts Scrooge is exposed to the importance of Christmas spirit, learning to foster it himself. He "did it all, and infinitely more."[7] **CONCLUSION** Thus, Scrooge's character is entirely reformed by the visits of the three spirits. Introduced in the first stave as a bitter and indignant businessman, Scrooge becomes in the final stave a man powered by compassion and gratitude.[8] Ultimately, it is through the teachings of the spirits that Scrooge's prolonged greed and ignorance erodes to give way to a revitalised Christmas spirit.	7. Here, the accompanying quote in the essay prompt has been addressed. If the quote has not been referenced in the introduction, it is important that it is touched on somewhere in the essay, even if the reference is very brief (as is the case here). 8. It is important to actually outline the specific changes in Scrooge's character. It is not enough to argue that he simply went from 'bad' to 'good'. Specific attitudes, values and characteristics should be identified.